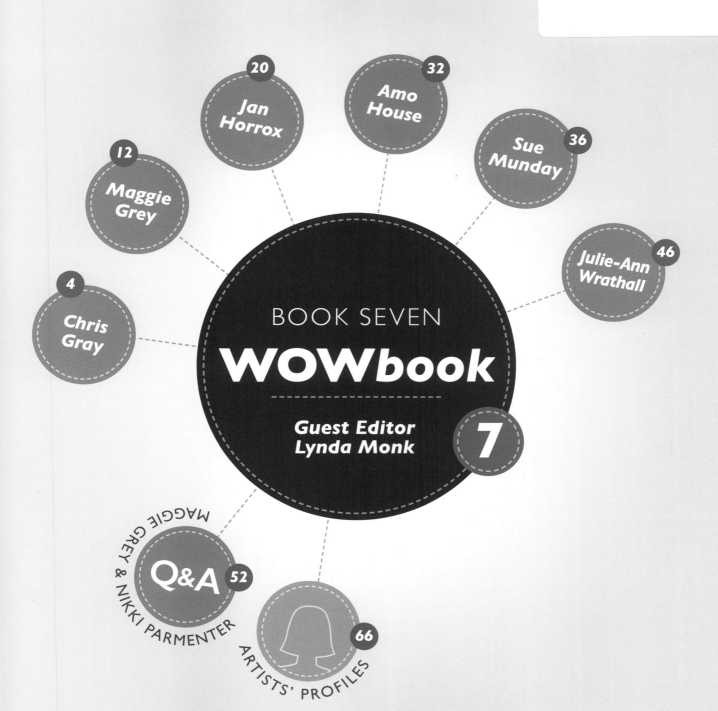

BOOK SEVEN

WOWbook

Guest Editor
Lynda Monk

7

Welcome to
WOWbook ❼
BOOK SEVEN

Is this really WOWbook 07? I truly can't believe that we have published six WOWbooks already! It's astonishing how time flies, even in these strange times. As I'm writing this, we are reflecting on a year of lockdown here in the UK. I don't think any of us expected that a year after the first lockdown, life would have changed so much.

I suppose one good thing has come out of it all. It's shown us how much we appreciate the little things — like meeting friends for a chat over coffee or popping to the shops. I really can't wait to do both of these things again.

Inspiration has been hard to find when we haven't been able to meet properly and discuss ideas, or take a trip to the annual shows and see the wonderful work of those exhibiting. I hope the WOWbooks have brought even just a tiny bit of inspiration your way.

Our Facebook group has been a great source of ideas. We love seeing the work you all produce from both the WOWbooks and from the online Members' Club — it's so inspiring to see how you take things further and in different directions. We are lucky to have so many of our contributors on hand to answer questions and give advice. Don't forget to check out the work in our Gallery at **wowbook.d4daisy.com.**

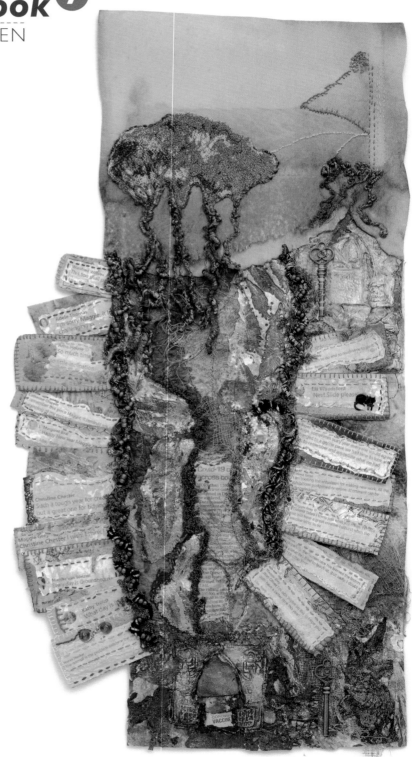

> *Lockdown* by Maggie Grey. This panel came about when Maggie asked her Facebook friends to leave comments about how they felt about being in lockdown and, with their permission, included them in the panel. The top of the panel is the calm landscape before Covid-19 and the 'golden river' (made from embossing powder) that runs through the piece represents the good aspects of social media. It runs down to an open door with the National Health Service (NHS) rainbow and a representation of the vaccine. Doors, open and shut, appear throughout the panel. They were formed from water-soluble paper.

We've spread the net far and wide to find the exciting workshops in this issue. We seem to have a little bit of everything – from building up an image using embossing powder, screen printing and stitch to creating *Medieval Fragments* with Chris Gray; a fabulous rubbing away technique for photo transfers with our very own Maggie; and Jan Horrox creating a cloth doll with a difference. Sue Munday manipulates images using the computer to then print and stitch, and Julie-Ann Wrathall is layering with encaustic wax and dammar. Finally, we persuaded Amo House to tell us about her fabulous temari balls. Hopefully, there's something for everyone here.

Maggie had a very informative chat with artist Nikki Parmenter about her work, and we are delighted to include the interview in this issue together with some of Nikki's beautiful art. Nikki has also written a workshop which you'll find in the online Members' Club for this WOWbook.

We hope this book gives you plenty of ideas and can't wait to see how you interpret the workshops. Come on over and join the chat in our Facebook group.

Lynda Monk

∨ Chris Gray. One of the double-page spreads from a small ring-bound book on a medieval theme. Chris used her wooden blocks to print onto the fabric and stitch around, then onto deli-paper for the left-hand page. Another tile printed from a rubber stamp tops it off with a little gold-leaf bling. To finish off the pages, edges were burnt and painted details added.

DIGGING FOR GOLD
Medieval Fragments

Chris Gray

We're all guilty of accumulating lots of 'stuff' throughout our creative lives – most of which we acquired because we thought it would be 'useful someday' or 'I can do something with that' or simply 'I want it!'. Unfortunately, much of it ends up lying around in drawers and boxes, never to see the light of day.

I am probably more guilty of this than most because I can tell myself that I need it for 'work' or to use for a workshop or an article and, over time, I find that I can hardly move in my workroom!

Writing this workshop for WOWbook provided me with the perfect time and opportunity to get digging and discover what lost stuff I could use.

As I am still in the throes of my long-lasting love affair with all things medieval, I decided to call this article *Medieval Fragments* because it is just that – a piece made from fragments, similar to the bits left over from the Middle Ages that are found all over the UK and Europe.

You may not have exactly the same materials lying around as I had, but just use whatever you can lay your hands on and enjoy the process. Being creative people, you will no doubt be able to find many ways of achieving a similar result but one that is more personal to you.

MATERIALS AND EQUIPMENT

- Canvas panel 8 × 8in (20 × 20cm)
- Tissue paper
- Glue (Mod Podge or PVA)
- Acrylic paint or printing ink
- Metallic acrylic paints or inks
- Handmade paper or silk noil paper
- Linen fabric 8 × 8in (20 × 20cm)
- Lightweight wadding/stabiliser
- Crackle paste
- Brusho-type spray
- Stencils – a fleur-de-lys design is used here
- Thermofax screen (optional)
- Photo transfer paper – inkjet or laser
- Wooden print blocks
- Various threads – variegated/metallic
- Thick felt or a piece of old blanket
- Fusible webbing
- Scrap paper
- Masking tape
- Double-sided tape
- Cardboard
- Paintbrushes and a spatula
- Sewing machine with free motion foot
- Book press or large books to use as a weight

> Finished piece *Medieval Fragments.*

TIP
You can create your own panel using any design you wish and many of the materials listed here can be substituted with similar products you may have in your workroom.

Preparing your canvas panel

The panel will be built up using a variety of techniques, including embossed paper and the photo transfer paper, which form the base area for additional techniques. The canvas panel will be the base for your piece and will be used when all the other steps have been completed. The canvas here measures 8 x 8in (20 x 20cm).

1. Take a piece of tissue paper and cut it to about 14 x 14in (35 x 35cm) – the inexpensive white tissue paper that comes with a new pair of shoes is ideal. Scrunch it up into a tight ball then carefully flatten it out again – but not so much as to lose all the wrinkles.

2. Using PVA glue or similar, brush the top surface of the canvas panel, covering it completely. Now take the wrinkled tissue paper and gently pat it down onto the glued surface and leave to dry.

3. Once the top is dry, repeat this process on the underside of the panel. Once again, leave overnight to dry completely.

4. Now spray the dry panel with brown Brusho and again, leave to dry. If you don't have brown Brusho in your stash, you could always use coffee grounds, tea or walnut ink decanted into a spray bottle.

5. Put the canvas panel to one side.

Print block embossing

1. Use double-sided tape to adhere the wooden print blocks to a piece of cardboard. This will prevent the blocks from moving when you carry out the next step in this process.

2. Cover the blocks with clingfilm to prevent the paper or fabric from sticking to the wood when pressed under a heavy weight.

3. Using the handmade paper, or silk noil, tear it to a size just a little larger than the blocks and spray well with yellow/brown Brusho to both colour and dampen the paper. This is necessary in order to achieve a good embossed finish.

4. Lay the paper, colour side down, on top of the blocks and cover with a piece of thick felt. The felt is needed to push the paper into the blocks' pattern recesses. Place this into a book press overnight. If you don't have a book press handy, a pile of heavy books will serve quite well.

5. The following day, remove the felt and carefully lift the paper from the blocks. It will still be damp, so leave to dry thoroughly. Once dry, put it to one side until you are ready to start stitching.

Preparing your linen background

Half of this background will be covered by the stitched transfer print – details below. The remainder of the panel will accommodate the embossed paper.

1. Choose a section of a detailed medieval pattern either from a book or from the internet (check copyright if you are likely to be selling your work). Print this onto a sheet of photo transfer paper. Use the photo transfer paper that relates to the printer you are using, either inkjet or laser. I used a drawing from one of my many medieval sketchbooks. This was taken from a stone carving on a Romanesque church and printed onto a piece of inkjet transfer paper.

   My image contained no text, so it didn't matter that the picture was reversed in the process. However, if you use an image that does contain text, you will need to flip it in an image manipulation program before printing it onto the transfer paper.

2. After printing, trim around the edges of the image. This will prevent a white border being visible.

3. Next, cut a piece of linen, slightly smaller than your prepared background canvas panel, and fray the edges to give an interesting finish.

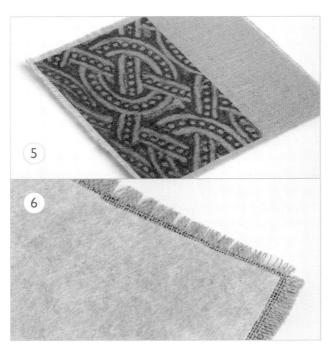

TIP
To achieve this result, you need a VERY hot iron and protection for your hands. The paper gets extremely hot and you can easily burn yourself if care is not taken. Use a small pair of pliers to grip the corner of the backing paper and peel it off in one go.

4. Lay the photo transfer print, face down, onto the linen and iron on the hottest setting to transfer the print to the fabric. Follow the manufacturer's instructions to obtain the best results.

5. Carefully peel the backing paper away while the image is still hot. This will give you a matt finish. If you prefer a gloss finish, leave the backing paper to cool completely before removing it.

6. Attach a piece of lightweight wadding to the back of your printed linen using a fusible webbing such as Bondaweb. This will add more depth to the finished piece, once you start stitching into the design.

7. Your linen panel is now ready for machine and hand stitching.

Time to stitch

1. Starting with the image on your linen piece, choose a suitably coloured variegated machine thread to stitch around the outlines. This can be done using straight machine stitching or free machine stitching, whichever you prefer.

2. In these photos below, the work was hand stitched with the same thread to create long straight stitches to infill the shaded areas.

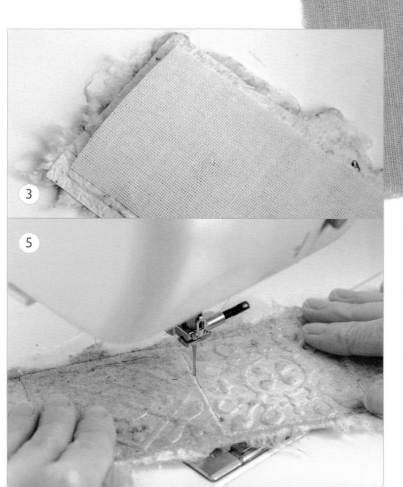

3. Taking your embossed paper image, iron a piece of stabiliser onto the back before stitching, to prevent tearing.

4. Thread the sewing machine with metallic thread and again, using straight or free machine stitching, stitch around the edges of the designs in the tiles.

5. When all the stitching has been completed, metallic acrylic paints or inks can be used to paint the raised areas. If you prefer, you can use a gilding wax here.

Screen printing

The next stage is to prepare the different areas for printing. You can use Thermofax screens, stencils or rubber/polymer stamps – whatever you have to hand.

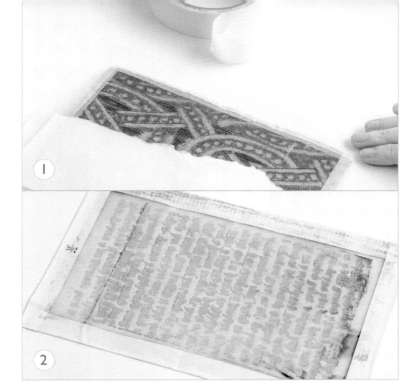

1. Take a piece of scrap paper and tear it into a rough-edged shape. Use masking tape to secure it to your linen background, leaving only part of the design visible. At the same time, add masking tape around the outside edges to ensure the printing doesn't go over the edges of your design.

2. This defined area can now be printed. I used black ink through a Thermofax screen with a medieval text design.

My design is a page taken from the *Red Book of Hergest* and is part of a story known as 'The First Branch of the Mabinogi', the story of Pwyll, Lord of Dyfed.

∧ Design printed onto sprayed tissue paper.

∧ Design printed onto the linen panel.

3. The ink should be allowed to dry completely before peeling away the scrap paper and masking tape, leaving the printed text.

Stencilling with crackle paste

Crackle paste is a dimensional white paste that creates an eggshell cracking pattern as it air-dries. This gives my work an aged look that I love.

1. A fleur-de-lys metal stencil was placed over the text printed area and all the unwanted sections were masked using small pieces of masking tape. As you can see, it took rather a lot of tiny pieces of masking tape to get it right!

2. Using crackle paste and a spatula, spread the paste liberally over your stencil.

3. Carefully lift the stencil off and leave to dry completely – overnight is perfect.

4. Once dry, the paste will have activated, leaving a crackled finish on the surface. You can now paint the tops of your shapes using a metallic acrylic paint.

5. To finish, glue your linen piece, together with your embossed tile piece, onto the prepared canvas panel.

Finishing

You may consider your panel finished, or you might like to add further embellishments — perhaps using some other pieces you may have come across in your stash.

I decided that my background needed a little more tweaking and, after a hunt around, I found another fleur-de-lys stencil that I had cut out using my Brother Scan'n'Cut machine. I also discovered some embossed paper fleur-de-lys shapes.

I stitched around the edges of the shapes and cut them out. Thin card or stiffened fabric could be used instead for an embellishment such as this.

Finally, a few fleurs-de-lys were stencilled onto the background panel using black metallic acrylic paint, and the two embossed pieces were glued into place.

My completed panel can be seen on page 5. You can create your own panel using any design you wish and with materials you have in your own stash.

> My finished piece *Medieval Fragments* (detail).

FADED GLORIES
Rubbing away photo transfers

Maggie Grey

I have been fascinated by frescos for many years and they have featured in much of my work. Visits to Italy, especially Pompeii, gave lots of opportunities for photographs and so provided my design source for this workshop.

Although some of the wall paintings are remarkably well preserved, my favourites are always the slightly faded ones and so they are very suitable for one of my favourite 'photo to fabric' techniques. I call this the 'rubbing away' method and it involves bonding a printout or photocopy face down onto a backing fabric, and then rubbing away the paper until you find the image underneath, fixed to the Bondaweb fusible webbing. You may lose a little of the detail but that just adds to the 'faded fresco' effect.

This method makes an ideal surface for works of faded glory, so, for this article, I have based the design on one of my photographs, of a fresco taken on holiday. There are many similar images online (but be aware of copyright issues). The transfer process will be described and I have chosen hand stitching on felt as a means of embellishment. The border effect gave the opportunity of further enhancement, which came by way of couched threads and stitched braids, combined with wrapped pipe-cleaners.

∧ *Oranges are the only fruit*. Hand-stitched piece based on a photograph of an Italian wall painting. It was printed and then bonded, upside down, to fabric before the paper was rubbed away to reveal the image. Hand stitching and a beaded border complete the look.

There are many ideas and techniques here that could be useful in other ways. I have found that this design transfer method, when worked on S80 Vilene, provides a great surface for machine embroidery. The braids could also be used to enhance cushions or garments – or even built up as vessels and book covers.

MATERIALS AND EQUIPMENT

- A printed image (inkjet, laser or photocopy) of your source material. Print on ordinary printer paper (not glossy). My image was 7 × 8in (18 × 20cm). It's best to print it a day or two before you need it.
- A piece of white felt, slightly larger than the printout
- Bondaweb fusible webbing
- Small sponge or paintbrush
- Embroidery silks or cottons in a variety of thicknesses
- Water-soluble film
- Yarns, ribbons, metal threads, machine threads
- Pipe-cleaners and beads that will slide onto them
- Usual sewing kit
- Sewing machine

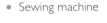

We will first look at the transfer of the design. I have suggested using felt as a background fabric as it is a good surface for hand stitching.

Design transfer

The stitched piece will feature the orange tree shown in the photo (with suitable supporting plant life) enhanced with couched thread and wrapped or stitched yarns.

1. First, print your image on ordinary printer paper. Use a 'High Quality' setting, if you can. Leave it for a couple of days for the ink to become stable. Cut it out with a 2in (5cm) border around it, then tear the edge of the paper a little so that it is slightly uneven.

2. Cut a piece of felt several inches/centimetres larger than your image. Cut a piece of Bondaweb fusible webbing slightly smaller than the felt.

3. Place the Bondaweb on the felt, paper side up, allowing a margin around the edge.

4. Iron the Bondaweb to the felt using a hot iron – make sure that it is well stuck, with no loose areas. If your felt is heat-reactive, make sure that you use non-stick backing paper under the iron. Peel off the Bondaweb backing.

5. Now lay the printout, **face down**, on top of the Bondaweb, cover with non-stick baking paper and iron it really well, with a hot iron. Again, check that it is well stuck. Leave for at least an hour, better still, overnight.

6. The next stage of the process involves gently painting or sponging water over the back of the paper. Don't make it too wet in one go – apply water in stages. You will see the image beginning to appear.

7. Now gently rub away the paper – sorry, but your finger will get grubby. Work through to the image layer which is stuck to the Bondaweb. You will see the colours begin to emerge and eventually, a faded version of the entire image will appear. You will probably find that it is all looking good while wet but, when it dries, the image is still obscured. It usually takes several more damping and rubbing away sessions until you are happy with the piece. It won't be quite as colourful as the original but that adds to the charm when working on a fresco theme. If you want a brighter image, rub with a small amount of cooking oil when dry.

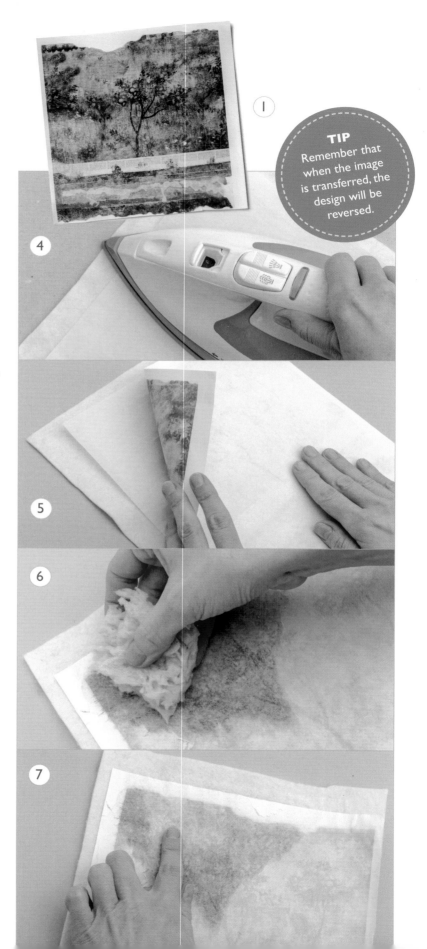

TIP
Remember that when the image is transferred, the design will be reversed.

When the piece is quite dry, you are ready to start adding stitch.

Stitching

Obviously your chosen photograph will be different from mine but I think the 'free stitching' style that I describe here would be suitable for a variety of backgrounds. Try making up your own variants of well-loved stitches. It's great fun. Simple straight stitches, free chain, straight and running stitch all work well. Make a small sampler, like mine, to see how the stitches and thread colours work together.

∨ Sampler to show how the stitches and thread colours work together.

^ Detail showing central tree with hand stitches. The 'oranges' are open chain stitch, the leaves are formed with straight stitches and the chunky tree trunk is also formed from small straight stitches.

I began with the orange tree which was worked with open chain stitch as follows.

Fruit

1. Form a chain in the usual way but don't pull the thread too tight.

2. Leave the stitch open and make a small stitch on each side of the chain to hold it open in a circle.

3. Fill the centre of the circle with small straight stitches, using a contrasting colour for the thread.

Leaves

The leaves are simply pairs of straight stitches worked around the oranges, using three colours of thread. It helps to vary the tone so I have used a yellowy-green and a mid-green with a few stitches in a darker green to add depth.

Trunk

The trunk was depicted in straight, horizontal stitches using tones of grey from almost white to dark grey. These stitches can be quite rough and chunky. An outline was then worked in a darker thread to define the shape. Further small stitches were taken across the trunk to suggest a gnarled appearance.

One other heavily stitched area was the shrub in the left foreground. This followed the stitching method used for the tree trunk, on a smaller scale, with 'free stitching' (just short, straight stitches) for the leaves.

The two orange trees on the right in the finished piece (see page 12) were not so well defined and I liked this shadowy effect, so minimal straight stitches and tiny free cross stitches were employed here. Paler thread colours gave a sense of perspective to set the trees in the background.

The final stitching for the main area of the piece was the stitching of a tracery of branches in the foreground above the border, using pale grey silks in two shades.

∨ Here you can see that the foliage and tree are almost complete and the border is beginning to take shape.

Lower border

One of the aspects that drew me to this particular photo was the faded border at the bottom of the design. A mix of formal stitches and machine-stitched braids combined well with an area of free stitching to prevent the border becoming too formal. I love using pipe-cleaners, wrapped with colourful threads or strips of fabric. Beaded chains would work here too and beads could be threaded onto the pipe-cleaners before wrapping.

∧ Detail of the border showing a variety of braids and wrapped pipe-cleaners.

TIP
Narrow pipe-cleaners are better for beading and wrapping but you can use a heat tool on the jumbo variety to slim them down.

Wrapped pipe-cleaners

Use a heavy hand-stitch yarn – I like a perlé – and simply tie it around the pipe-cleaner, just in from the end. Now begin to wrap, covering the end of the thread as you wind. Build up 'bumps' in places as you go along. Cut the thread at the end and stitch it down securely.

You could also try threading some chunky beads onto the pipe-cleaner before you begin wrapping. Just jump the thread over the bead as you go along. If the beads have very tiny holes, try threading them on wire instead. My finished piece shows some freshwater pearls threaded on thin wire and then wrapped. This gave a great shape. Making braids and wrappings is good fun. I make lots in one session for my 'bits cupboard' and they are often just what you need to finish a piece of work.

< A variety of braids and wrapped pipe-cleaners, suitable for building up the lower border.

< Braids made by machine stitching yarns on water-soluble paper.

Here's how ...

Set up the sewing machine on its widest zigzag stitch and then gather together three or four thick threads, one of them glitzy – I used a flat gold braid here.

Lay the threads on the water-soluble fabric and pin them into position. If you are nervous about stitching over the pins, remove them as you reach them. Stitch with the foot on, using a suitable bobbin and top thread, remembering that the bobbin thread will show. Use your widest zigzag. If your machine only offers the option of a narrow zigzag, just work two rows, side by side. If you have some interesting patterns, work a further line or two of stitch on top of the zigzag. Experiment to find the best stitch width for the effect you want.

∧ Yarns, machine stitched on water-soluble fabric, which was washed away after stitching. Goldwork threads add an irresistible gleam.

Machine-stitched braids

I thought that there was fun to be had in adding a bit of glitz to reconstruct a little of the faded glory that would almost certainly be present in the original. Not wanting it to be too perfect, I used a method of braid-making that the late Val Campbell-Harding and I devised together, many years ago, for a machine embroidery class. It involves stitching a variety of heavy threads and yarns onto water-soluble fabric and working zigzag stitch or patterns over them. When the soluble backing is dissolved away, a slightly untidy braid is revealed.

When the border was stitched, I had to make a great decision – should I tea-stain the edges by dabbing the white felt border with a teabag? I often do this as I love the way the tea seeps into the printed area of the design, making a soft edge. If you go for it – as I did – just pour boiling water over a teabag until it comes up to the middle of the mug. Hook the teabag out straight away, minding your fingers. Now keep the mug handy and allow the teabag to cool. Squeeze it a little before dabbing gently around the edges, starting from the outside – don't make it too wet. Keep an eye on the teabag – if it looks as though it might explode, wet another one. When you've been all the way round, allow the work to dry before folding the top and bottom edges to the back and securing with a few rows of running stitch to hold it in place.

∨ Detail showing how a tea stain can be used to define an edge.

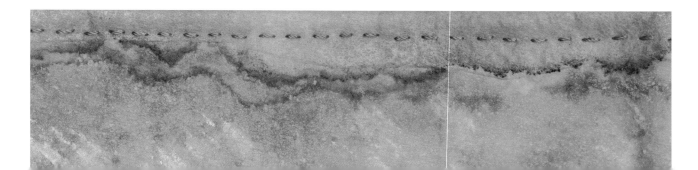

At this stage, the work could be considered complete. With the side edges folded and stitched – or trimmed or singed with a soldering iron – it could be conventionally framed. However, the side edges had curled under in a scroll-like fashion, which I really liked. So a decision was made to emphasise this with the sides of the work gently rolled over short lengths of bamboo and the piece placed on a painted, textured background. The 'scroll' was popped in a deep frame and secured with double-sided tape.

I did enjoy making this piece, especially the unexpected advent of the scroll – I do love a happy accident.

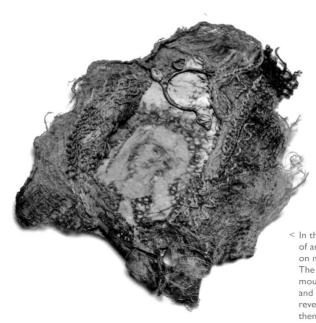

< In this piece, my drawing of an icon was made on much thinner paper. The ethereal image was mounted on metal shim and rubbed away to reveal the face. It was then machine stitched to Kozo fibre and hand-stitched. Do try the transfer technique with a variety of fabrics and weights of paper.

< Finished piece framed as a scroll. A variety of effects can be achieved with this technique.

LOVE GROWS WHERE MY ROSEMARY GOES
Making a cloth doll

Jan Horrox

Art dolls are iconic artefacts. Historically, in many ancient cultures they were treasured objects.

Modern cloth dolls feature in today's textile art and craft world as an exciting vehicle for all kinds of technique providing the opportunity to create a unique doll of your own.

As textile designer/makers we all have a collection of fabrics: given, bought and found. Doll-making is an ideal project for re-purposed fabrics. They use small pieces so having a large variety to select from is really helpful and it's exciting to put together a number of pieces for your doll.

The doll I have created for this workshop is themed on the idea of 'earth' and, in particular, herbs and spices. At the forefront of my theme is climate change. As we stand upon the brink, and muse about our future, now is the time to make your own heirloom doll to pass on to the world. I have reflected this theme in creating this doll and by using eco-dyed fabrics. There is a wonderful workshop by Caroline Bell in WOWbook 01 which tells you how to create these fabrics. The embroidery represents the roots in the earth and I have made the hair using natural dyed fibre in earthy colours.

This project is a simple cloth doll. The doll is 15in (38cm) tall with a basic sculpted face, drawn features and stitched joints. Using your own choice of textures and colours, you can use these instructions and templates to create your own interpretation of a unique doll.

> My finished doll, *Rosemary*, one of my latest series of dolls based on herbs and spices.

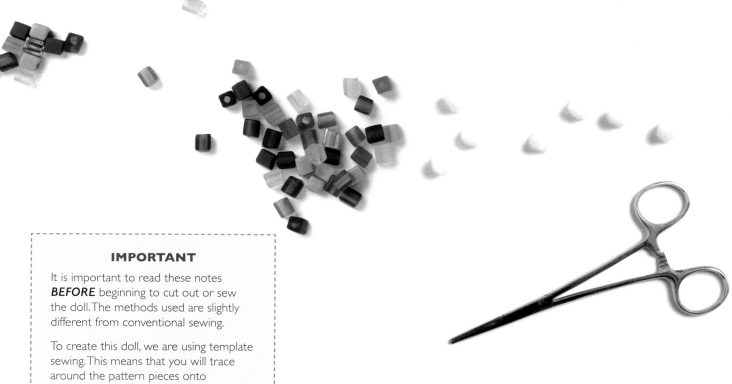

MATERIALS AND EQUIPMENT

- Flesh fabric – a quilting quality, A4 size
- Fabric for arms, legs and body. Use the templates to find a suitable size. All pieces should be cut on double fabric.
- Chiffon – a scarf or a piece
- Organza
- Polyester toy filling
- Wensleydale locks (curly wool)
- Cotton pompom × 10mm
- Chenille sticks 6mm × 4
- Forceps – about 5in (12cm) or a chopstick
- Small sharp embroidery scissors
- Long doll needle 6in (15cm) approx.
- Long darning needle – I used a size 7
- Threads – quilting thread for sculpting and jointing; machine sewing thread and hand embroidery threads
- Coloured pencils – watercolour pencils, used dry
- 2B sharp drawing pencil
- White gel pen
- Glass headed pins
- Open embroidery foot
- Needle-felting needle 38/40

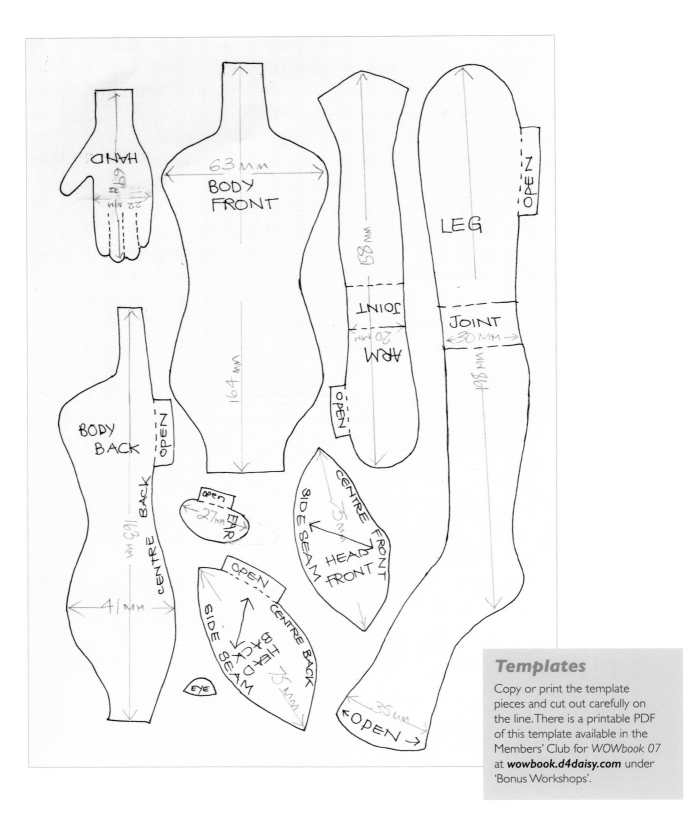

HAND
69 mm
22 mm

BODY FRONT
63 mm
164 mm

ARM
JOINT
158 mm
20 mm
OPEN

LEG
OPEN
JOINT
30 mm
108 mm

BODY BACK
OPEN
CENTRE BACK
169 mm
41 mm

EAR
open
27 mm

HEAD FRONT
CENTRE FRONT
SIDE SEAM
75 mm

HEAD BACK
OPEN
CENTRE BACK
SIDE SEAM
75 mm

EYE

OPEN
35 mm

Templates

Copy or print the template pieces and cut out carefully on the line. There is a printable PDF of this template available in the Members' Club for WOWbook 07 at *wowbook.d4daisy.com* under 'Bonus Workshops'.

Making the doll

Head

1. Use the flesh-coloured fabric, folded double.
   Place the head templates onto this fabric with
   the grain line parallel to the selvedge. Mark
   around these pieces with a pencil. This is the
   stitching line. Please note the cross marking
   on the top of both head templates and mark
   this on the fabric.

2. Machine stitch the centre front and centre
   back seams as marked on the template. Leave
   the back opening, where marked. Now mark
   a 1cm seam allowance on the two side seams.
   Cut out these two pieces for the head, with
   a 4mm allowance on the stitched seams. Flip
   these pieces over, replace the template and
   mark the stitching line on this side of the
   two pieces. You now have all the stitching
   lines marked.

3. Pin these two pieces together, matching the
   marked stitching lines all around and with the
   seams at the top and bottom placed together.
   Make sure you have the back and front of the
   head the same way up – the cross markings
   should be together. It is very easy to stitch
   these together with one piece the wrong way
   up. If you do, then your face will never be the
   right shape. Machine all around the side seams
   in one go – make sure not to catch a pleat
   anywhere at the top or bottom of the head.

4. Trim the side seams to 4mm. Pull the head
   right way out through the back opening using
   your forceps. Put the pompom into the nose
   shape on the front profile and pin in place.
   This gives such a nice nose shape which is
   difficult to achieve otherwise. Fill the head
   with stuffing using your forceps or a chopstick.
   Make a nice firm head with a good even
   shape. The weight of a fully stuffed head is
   approximately 12g.

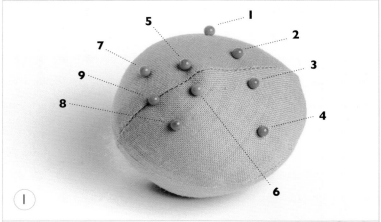

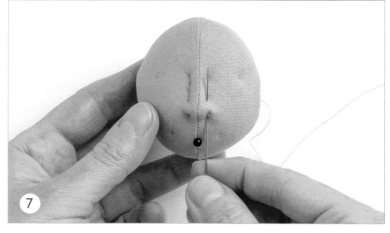

Sculpting the head

Now that you have made the head, you can sculpt the features to create a 3D face.

1. Place the pins as shown, 1cm between the pins for the bridge of the nose: **2** and **3**.

2. Leave 1.3cm for your pin at outer edge of the eye: **1** and **4**.

3. You need two pins for the nostrils: **5** and **6**.

4. You need three pins for the mouth: **7**, **8** and **9**.

5. Take a long darning needle and a length of quilting thread or strong thread. Attach to the back of the head and push the needle through the head and out at 3. Go back in the same place, making a small stitch of a few threads, and out at 2. This makes the bridge of the nose. Make a few stitches back and forth and pull firmly to create the bridge of the nose.

6. Continue to stitch down the nose from side to side, pulling with each stitch to form the nose. Stop about 7.5mm above the nostrils above pin 6.

7. Push the needle in from the last stitch so that it exits out of the nostril (6) then back in with a small stitch and out on your original stitch. Stitch across to the other side of the nose above pin 5 and repeat the process. This creates the nose.

8. Push the needle in at the same place and out at pin 1. Take a small stitch then back in and out at pin 8. Make a small stitch and back in, then out again at pin 4. Back in and out again at pin 7. Lastly, make a small stitch and take the needle out of the back of the head and fasten off. With each stitch, pull quite firmly to make a small sculpted dip to be used when drawing the face.

Drawing and colouring the face

1. Use a sharp 2B pencil to draw the features. Fit the eye template between the two sculpting stitches for the eye. Pin here and draw an outline for the eye. Flip over for the other eye and draw in place.

2. Draw in the iris and the pupil of the eyes within the outline. Draw in the eyelid and eyebrow for both eyes.

3. Draw in the centre line of the mouth and then add the upper line and lower line of the mouth. It's a good idea to practise drawing the features on some paper before drawing onto the fabric. You can erase the pencil lines with a good-quality eraser but don't do this too much.

4. The colours I used for the face are pencil crayons in warm grey, yellow ochre, burnt ochre, black grape, scarlet and ultramarine. I also used a white gel pen.

5. I added warm grey around the eye sockets and down the sides of the nose and black grape above the eyelid. Yellow ochre was added under the eye and scarlet lightly on the cheeks. I drew scarlet on the lips and then more pencil lines around the eyes and mouth to define the shape.

6. I used ultramarine for the iris and a white gel pen for the highlights and whites of the eyes.

7. Use a scrap of fabric to blend the colours together and into the fabric.

8. You should try out all of this on some spare fabric first. In fact, it's a good idea to make two heads and use one to practise on.

9. Use these photos as a guide to improvise and create your own face.

Making the ears

Using fabric folded double, draw around the ear template twice. Stitch around the drawn outline, leaving the opening. Cut out both pieces with a 4mm allowance. Pull both through to the right side and insert a small amount of stuffing. You can hand stitch a line around the inner ear, as I have done here. Push in the turnings and stitch in place onto the side of the head. The top of the ear should be level with the eye.

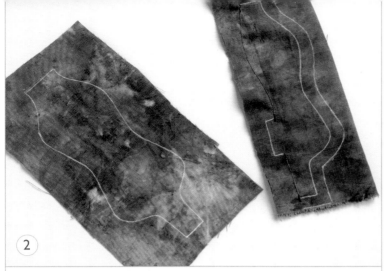

(2)

(3)

Making the body

1. Using fabric folded double, draw around the body back template. Stitch the centre back seam, leaving the opening. Mark a 10mm seam allowance around the side seams. Cut out with a 4mm seam allowance on the centre back stitched seam and a 10mm allowance on the side seams.

2. Place the front body template onto single fabric and trace around. Mark a 10mm seam allowance all the way around. Cut out on the outer line.

3. Pin both of the body pieces together, matching the stitching lines. Stitch all the way around and trim the seam to 4mm. Pull the right way out through the opening. Stuff through the opening until firmly and evenly filled. Make sure to fill the neck, shoulders and hips very firmly, as the limbs and head need to be strongly supported. The weight of the body when finished is approximately 20g.

Hands

1. On fabric folded double, draw around the hand template to make two hands. Stitch around, leaving the wrist open. Cut out with a 4mm seam allowance. Clip the seam in between the thumb and hand and pull to the right side.

2. Using the hand template, draw in the lines for the fingers. Top stitch either by hand or machine.

3. Take the chenille sticks and cut into 6in (15cm) lengths. Bend in half and bend down the sharp ends with forceps. Push the chenille sticks into the fingers, with one end in each finger, and a double chenille stick in the thumb. Using forceps, push a small amount of stuffing into the palm of each hand. Make sure you have a left and a right hand. Trim the ends of the chenille sticks level with the wrists. With a darning needle and quilting thread, put three sculpting stitches into each hand to form the knuckles.

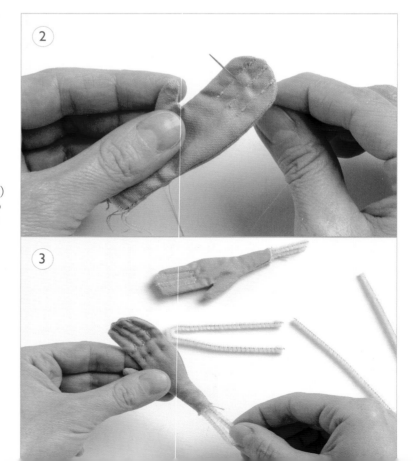

(2)

(3)

Arms

1. On fabric folded double, trace around the arm template twice. Stitch around, leaving the wrist open. Trim the seams to 4mm and pull both arms through to the right side. Mark the position for both lines (marked on the template for the joint), with some tacking stitches on the right side of the fabric. Stuff the top of the arm to just above the marks for the joint. Stitch a gathering thread around both of these lines, gather and tie off. This will keep the top arm stuffing in place.

2. Fill the lower arm with stuffing to just above the wrist. This needs to be firm, but with enough space to push the finished hand into the wrist. Both arms should be completed at this stage so that you can fit the hands at the same time to ensure they match. You will probably need to adjust the amount of stuffing in the lower arm, so that the hand will fit into the wrist properly. You can see from the photo (right) how far the hand has gone into the wrist. The wrist will overlap the hand down to the knuckle. Pin the hand in place.

3. Now we are going to use embroidery thread to add some running stitches down the outside of the arm. I used two strands of embroidery floss. Fasten in the top of the arm and stitch down to the joint markers. Wind the thread you are using around the joint a number of times down to the lower mark, continuing down the lower arm and the wrist to attach the hand to the arm. Repeat this as many times as you like, winding each thread around the joint. When you have finished the side of the arm, put a few stitches on the inside of the wrist to secure the hand. Complete both arms so they are the same. The weight of the finished hand and arm is approximately 6g.

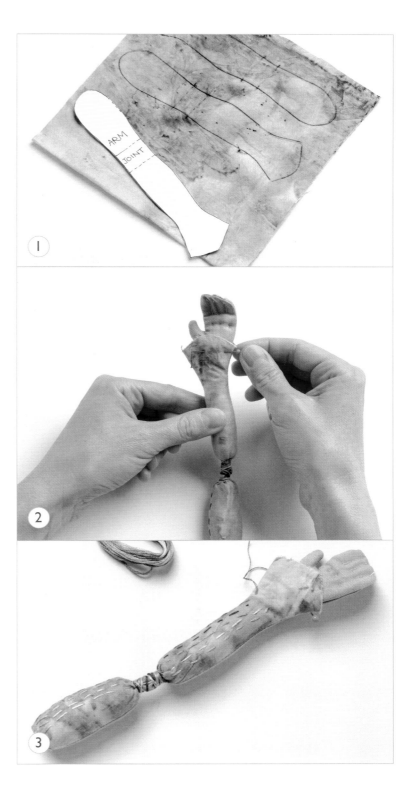

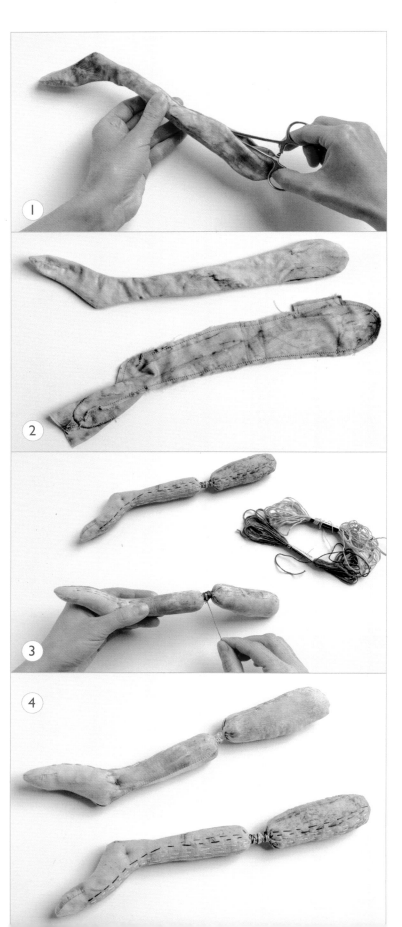

Legs

The legs are made in a similar way to the arms, except for the toe shape.

1. On fabric folded double, draw around the template and stitch around, leaving the opening on the thigh as well as the toe. Cut out with a 4mm seam allowance on the stitched seam and a 10mm allowance for the toe.

2. Pin the toe seams together and mark a rounded toe shape, as shown on photo (left). Stitch around this shape and trim to a 4mm allowance. Pull through to the right side. Using the template, mark the two joint lines onto the right side of the leg fabric with a thread – but do not gather yet.

3. Stuff the toes, feet and ankles up to the joint marker. Make sure you have a firm foot and ankle for each leg. Pull up the two threads for the joint and fasten off. Now stuff the top of the legs through the opening and close the opening with a very neat stitch. The weight of each finished leg is approximately 14g.

4. Using embroidery thread and a running stitch, as you did for the arms, attach at the top of the thigh. On the outside of the leg, stitch down to the joint, wind around the joint a few times and then continue with running stitch down to the foot. Add as many lines of stitching as you like. You need the joint to be well covered with thread.

Jointing limbs to the body

Both the arms and legs are jointed onto the body in the same way. You will need a long doll needle about 5in (12cm) long, some strong quilting thread and four beads.

1. Attach a long thread to the seam of the body, in the curve of the hip where the leg will fit. Line up both the legs with the toes facing forwards. Pass through the top of the leg, through the bead, back through the leg, through the body and out the other side in line with the entry point, through the top of the leg, through the bead, back through the top of the leg and back through the body to where you started. You will see you have both legs anchored to the hip of the body with thread and a bead on either side so that the legs can move naturally. Pull this thread to put tension on the joint. Repeat twice and pull each time to give that tension on the joint so that the legs do not swing freely. Fasten off at the back of one of the legs with a few small stitches.

2. Attach the arms in exactly the same way, making sure that the thumbs are pointing to the front and the hands are palm inwards.

Fitting the head to the neck

With your forceps, make a space inside the opening at the back of the head. Push the neck into this opening. Pin in place and stitch very neatly around the join.

Adding hair

I have used dyed Wensleydale locks for my doll's hair and have needle-felted it into the head.

1. Usually the locks come with a curly end and a felted end, tied in bundles. Untie and divide into separate locks. If the felted end is too bulky, trim it down.

2. Hold the felted end of the lock against the head and needle-felt in place. Continue to add more locks and needle-felt in place to cover the head, creating a hairstyle as you go. If you don't like it, just ease the locks out and redo. Continue with this until you have a lovely head of hair. Over time, the locks can become loose. If this happens, just re-felt them back into place. This is a great way of creating hair for a cloth doll. You can use any fibres you like.

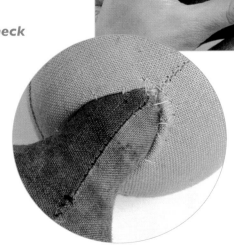

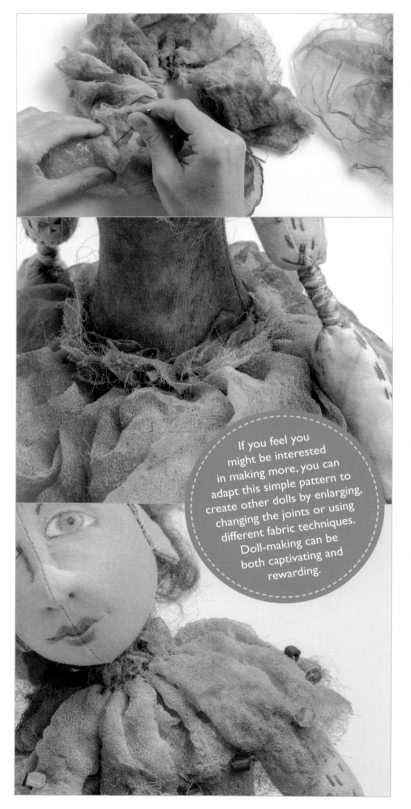

Clothes

For a simple costume I have created a two-layer skirt and a ruff around the neck.

1. For the underskirt, I used a piece of synthetic organza 4 × 23½in (10 × 60cm) which I heated with a heat tool to create texture. This gives some bulk to the chiffon skirt, which is on top. Run a gathering thread along one of the long sides and pull up to fit around the hips of the doll. Pin in place and tack with small stitches.

2. For the top skirt, I used a piece of chiffon 7 × 31½in (18 × 80cm) which I distressed with a needle-felting needle. To do this, place the chiffon on a piece of folded bubblewrap or some sponge and attack with the needle. If you have a four-needle tool or, even better, an embellishing machine, you can randomly use it to create a texture. Distress this to your satisfaction. I frayed the hem edge.

   As with the underskirt, run a gathering thread along one long side and gather around the hips on top of the organza skirt. Stitch in place with some beads.

3. The ruff or collar is a piece of chiffon 4 × 16in (10 × 40cm) which was distressed in the same way. Fold lengthways and gather along the folded edge. I have frayed the raw edge and stitched beads along this edge. Pull up the gathers and fit around the neck. Stitch in place.

You now have a finished doll.

If you feel you might be interested in making more, you can adapt this simple pattern to create other dolls by enlarging, changing the joints or using different fabric techniques. Doll-making can be both captivating and rewarding.

> *Rosemary*, my finished doll, on the theme of herbs and spices.

TURNING JAPANESE
My take on temari balls

Amo House

For the past few years, when creating things, I have been trying to use what I have in my stash already, only adding to it when there really is no alternative. I have also been randomly choosing a bundle of things, then trying to work out what to do with them. It's proved interesting!

Recently, my 'storeroom' had to be made ready for a guest and, during the tidy-up, an old, dusty basket of balls, threads and tights used to make temari balls many, many years ago, was unearthed.

The word *temari* is Japanese for 'handball'. They were originally made from leather for boys to play with. Women soon realised that they could produce more delicate ones for their daughters with scraps of old silk kimonos. This, in turn, was a way of the women showing off their sewing skills, and they became treasured gifts from a parent.

Temari balls are made from little card cubes which are packed with a wish and some rice to create a rattle. The cubes are then placed in a piece of stocking which is carefully stuffed with leftover bits of yarn. That is then heavily and tightly wrapped with more yarn, making sure to keep it all spherical.

Finally, cotton thread is tightly wound over the yarn to give the temari ball a base. For this final layer, the colour is important. It is these threads that the decorative stitches are worked into. The finished ball is surprisingly firm if you have done it right.

At one time, I made quite a few and gave them away, hoping to make many more. But something must have distracted me, as these things do, and the basket was put away. They are quite time-consuming to make and, if you look them up on the internet, often exceedingly intricate.

∧ Traditional and stitched temari balls.

∨ Two of my original, traditionally stitched temari balls – luckily rescued from the dog!

∨ A collection of old and newly-stitched temari balls.

After hunting around the house, I found a couple of my completed balls, followed by a third a few days later. I can remember having them on display. We had a new rescue dog at the time (we've now had her for six years) who thought they were great fun to play with and she made a real mess with them. These three were all that were left and I thought I might use the found parts to make some more. But did I really still have the patience needed for the real, full-on temari ball process?

One day before Christmas, I was reading through some blogs and saw that Sandra of Wild Daffodil (*www.daffodilwild.wordpress.com*) had been playing with some of her grandchildren's play balls by covering them with silk scraps and teabag paper. Balls are balls, so I thought — why not cover my finished balls with something other than the intricate stitches they should have?

They were on my work desk for a while before inspiration started to filter in. My first choice was to couch some chenille thread in random patterns around one of them. When completed, I wasn't too impressed with the result, so put that aside and began stitching fishbone stitch over a second one. This is a stitch I had recently learnt while doing some crewelwork. It's self-padding and makes a lovely raised leaf shape. All the yarns used were leftovers from past projects that needed using up or to be thrown away. A few beads were added to give a bit more texture and life to the ball, and it was finished.

∧ I have couched chenille threads down onto the ball to make cell shapes, which I have then filled with fabric. These are (left to right) lace, twine-wrapped, traditionally made and silk-pieced temari balls.

∨ For this temari ball, I used fishbone stitch and beads in autumn colours to cover the entire ball.

∧ Linen stitched with a toadstool and encrusted with stitches wrapped around the ball.

While looking through a drawer, I came across a piece of linen I had stitched into a toadstool and had then embellished the background with stitches. It was a nice piece of work but living in a drawer. It was the perfect size to wrap around a ball and all the encrusted stitches meant the seams and darts needed to make it fit were hidden. This is probably my favourite ball as there is so much to look at.

> Monochrome silks and chiffons stitched and added to continue the patterns.

For my next ball, I chose to cover it in some black and white silk scraps. There were lovely patterns on the silk which were used as a starting point. While stitching this ball, I decided to go back to a previous ball where I had couched chenille threads down onto the ball to make cell shapes, and to fill in the cells with pieces of metallic lace, hand-dyed velvet and stitch.

> Tiny squares of silk were cut out using pinking shears and layered with pink silk and chiffon in graduating colours. Finally, this ball was held together by a dressmaking pin pushed all the way through.

In one of those strange little boxes we all have, I discovered a full container of steel dressmaking pins. I can't remember the last time I used that type. Having just trimmed the winter heads off of my hydrangeas and thinking of the lovely bracts, I chose some recycled silks. Pinking shears were used to cut squares of about 1cm, in colours from palest green to palest pink. Each square was layered up with a bright pink piece of silk and a piece of pink chiffon. An orange bead was added to the pin, which was pushed through the three layers of silk into the ball. By choosing the colours carefully, the ball has a gradual colour change. This was linked to the others by its pink centre.

∧ Old, unloved sequins having their time to shine in the creation of this colourful temari ball.

∧ Plain hemp garden twine receives an uplift to produce this decorative temari ball.

The next ball was just a riot. A pot of old, unloved sequins finally had their time to shine! I managed to find quite a rhythm stitching these, which did take a bit of time. This one is a total contrast to all the others and I'm pleased with the end result. And on the plus side, another thing that I've had for years has been used.

The last stitched temari ball is made from hemp twine, the kind you find in a garden centre. This ball of twine lived in the studio, tangling itself up with plenty of other things and never quite managing to make it back out into the garden. A variegated perlé thread was used to stitch it down in a spiral, with a centre band in a contrast colour for interest.

My finished temari balls are now displayed together in a tall glass vase where they can all be seen, not stuck in a drawer and unloved. I am so pleased that I managed to use up materials that could so easily have been discarded. Looking at things in a different light can open all sorts of doors. What have you got that could be used in another way?

> A selection of my temari balls. They make an eye-catching display, adding a 'pop' of colour to any room, and are no longer unloved in a drawer.

ARCHING BACK
Image manipulation, Thermofax printing and stitch

Sue Munday

It had been a long hard winter and a visit to the county of Kent, UK, for Easter did not seem like a good prospect. However, Mother Nature thought otherwise. The sun shone and the leaves unfurled, the rape fields blossomed and people threw off their clothes (to sit on the beach, I may say).

At the beginning, we went into Canterbury Cathedral, where the old water tower – the oldest part of the building – drew my attention. Arches and more arches, words engraved on a stone in the gardens, repeating patterns – and so my ideas began. As I usually do when away on our travels, I kept a journal, making notes of the places we visited, people we met, and adding my own photos. I also noted the sounds heard – the birds, the sea and the rustling of the leaves on the trees.

I like to combine images to stitch, be it hand, free machine or using digitising software on the computer. I have also thrown a little Thermofax printing into the mixing pot.

If you're not into computer design, this workshop can used with your existing Thermofax screens.

MATERIALS AND EQUIPMENT

- Lutradur 30 or 70
- Calico for the background
- Stitch-n-Tear or similar stabiliser
- Machine threads to suit your project
- Bubble Jet Set 2000. This is a complex resin formula designed to make permanent images on fabric when using an inkjet printer
- Thermofax screen – either your own or a purchased design
- Screen-printing inks (I get mine from *www.screens4printing.com*)
- Canvas mount in a suitable size for your work
- Images – I used my own photographs taken at Canterbury Cathedral
- Corel Paint Shop Pro, Adobe Photo or similar program

> *Canterbury.* My completed panel constructed using screen-print combined with computer design and stitch techniques.

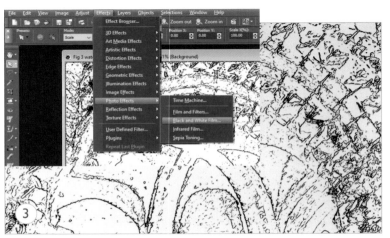

Creating your image

1. For my piece, I experimented with the effects on my image in Corel Paint Shop Pro.

   The arch was created using the Fresco effect, plus Faded Edges. You will see by the screenshot here, that I used Effect then Fresco, then Faded Edges on my computer. Remember to save as you go along, just in case you lose one of your experiments.

2. Next, using my photograph of the arch, I altered this using Effects, then Glowing Edges, and then selecting Invert which removes all colour and leaves a wonderful skeletonised image.

3. I created a black and white image for my Thermofax screen by choosing Effects, then black and white. When I was happy with the results, I sent this to *www.screens4printing.com*.

4. Returning to the image in point 2 above, I used the Freehand Selection tool to remove the hard edges. This would translate well to fabric where you could use a soldering iron or a sharp pair of scissors on printed Lutradur.

5. I also took a photo of a decorative pillar. The pillar was created with Effects-Artistic Effects-Coloured Edges. Now is the time to experiment until you are happy. Remember to save as you go along.

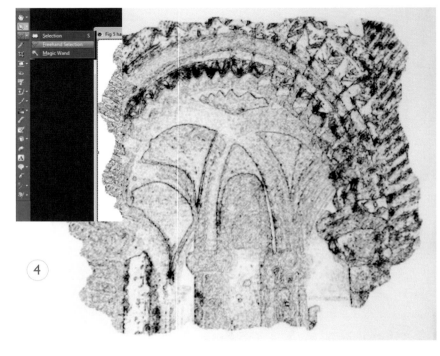

6. A section from the top of the pillar was taken from the previous image as a background for the design. The shape was taken into my digitising software and stitches created. This could also be worked with free machine stitch but I do like to experiment with my computer.

7. I took the shape from the top of the carved pillar and repeated it. By taking the image of the pillar into my embroidery software, I was able to trace over the decorative shape, thereby replicating the lovely scrolled leaf design. I then created the repeat pattern by mirror imaging the original design selection. I first stitched out a trial sample on calico and, when satisfied, I printed out the design from my software. This enabled me to position it correctly, using the crosshair marks to position it, then I stitched it onto my piece of pillar-printed Lutradur.

8. Working on my photograph of the interior of the Cathedral, I reduced the colour of the image to blend in with my background and altered the hard edge.

9. While exploring, I spotted a large stone decorated with words in the Cathedral gardens and decided to use them in this piece of work. I used the lettering facility in the embroidery software to create the words in two parts. These were stitched onto the body of work, once the Lutradur images were attached.

5

6

7a

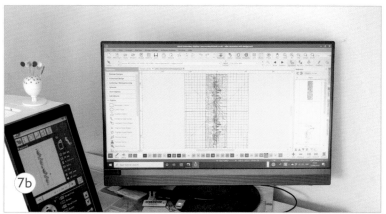

7b

8

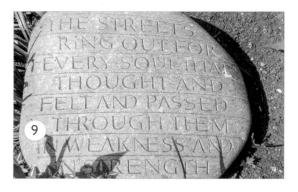

9

Screen printing

Once I received the Thermofax screen, it was essential to ensure the screen worked well, and this image was my test print.

1. Choose your colours to suit your photos so that your piece has a colour theme. The calico background was coloured with screen-printing inks, but you could use acrylics if you prefer. Remember to dampen the calico first to allow the colours to mingle. I use a spray bottle filled with water to achieve this. I printed on spare fabric to check the print before using my prepared background fabric.

2. Place your screen ready to hand and select the colours you plan to use. Mix your colours together using an old plate or palette (or a Gelli plate). I chose the primary colours – red, blue and yellow – with white and black to give tones. I mixed the colours to achieve my required final colour using these primaries.

   Once you have achieved your desired colour, you are ready to go. Remember to have a trial run first on a spare piece of fabric or paper. If you have not attempted this before, there are many videos on YouTube (printing with Thermofax screens). Alternatively, there are several books available.

3. First, cover your printing base with plastic or newspaper to protect it. An old blanket is a good idea, as this helps the transference of the image, giving a soft base for the fabric.

4. Screen print over the coloured background. This gives a good base to your images and blends them. Remember to keep a bowl full of water nearby, large enough to fit your screen. Pop the screen in as soon as you have completed the printing so that the ink/paint doesn't dry, then clean it off with a sponge.

5. I applied colour to the top of the Thermofax screen by dragging the colour from left to right in a line across the top of the screen image, ready for using the scraper to drag the colour from top to bottom of the screen.

   Just try it – you will have lots of fun. One photo or image can be extended in many ways, by printing, stitching or just taking a part of it to extend and develop.

6. Lift your Thermofax screen carefully to one side to see your printed image.

< Test print from my Thermofax screen.

> When you are happy with the result, screen print over the painted calico.

Printing

Once you have prepared your base fabric, by colouring and Thermofax screen printing, you can print off your images on paper. This helps you plan your work. By moving the printed paper images around, you can get the feel and the balance right. When you are happy that the prints work on the background, you can print them on Lutradur using an inkjet printer.

1. Prepare the Lutradur by soaking it in Bubble Jet Set 2000 in an old baking tray. Dry overnight by suspending the Lutradur by a peg or similar, allowing the excess to drip back into your tray. This can then be returned to the bottle and re-used.

2. Print your images from your computer onto the prepared Lutradur. To make this easier for your printer, use either freezer paper to support the Lutradur, or an A4 sticky label. The printer will love you. Remember to do a test run first to decide which way up your Lutradur needs to be.

3. Ensure that your Lutradur is cut to A4 size for your printer and your A4 label.

4. Remove the backing from the sticky label.

5. Lay your Lutradur down on a smooth surface, and carefully apply the label, sticky side down.

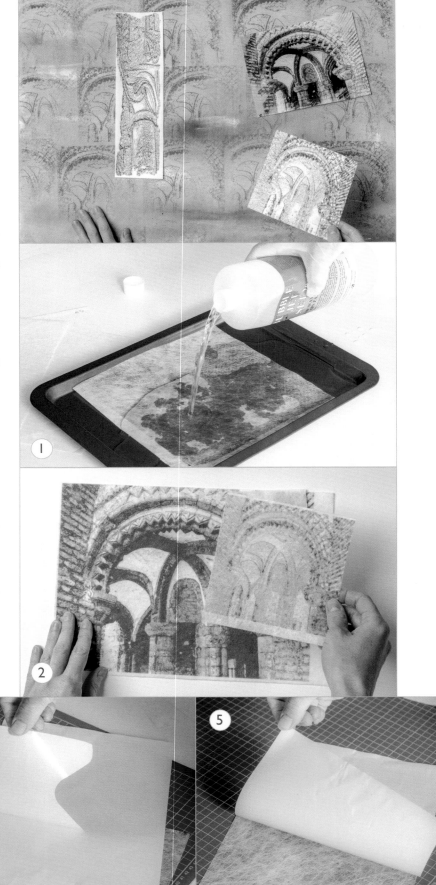

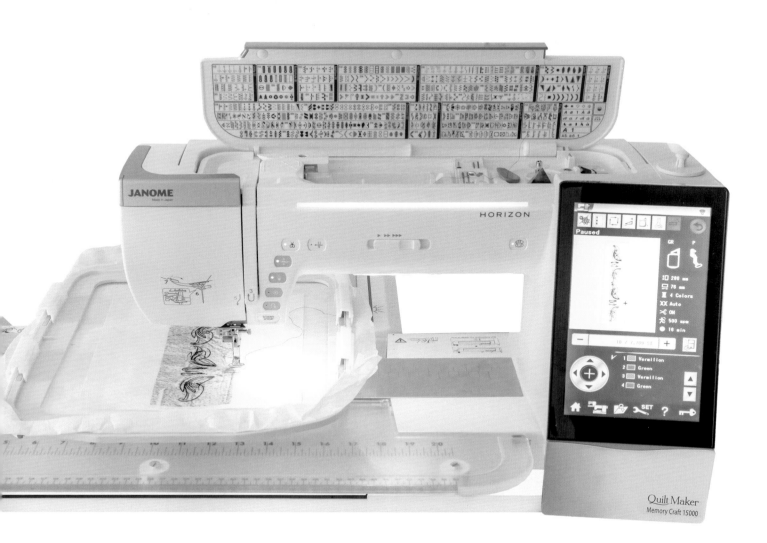

∧ My machine with the stabiliser hooped securely. The Lutradur pillar image has been taped down and then the outline stitched. Finally, the decorative design was stitched onto it.

Stitching

Once your Lutradur is printed, you can start stitching into it, either as I have or by using free machine stitching. I have, of course, used my digitising software to create arch shapes, by scanning my images into the software. This has allowed me to digitise shapes into stitches. I have stitched into some of my images using the digitised design and the embroidery machine. I have also free machine stitched the Lutradur images securely onto the background fabric before stitching into them.

Putting it all together

1. Assemble your photographs and stitched pieces and apply to the background.

2. Lay your background fabric on a flat surface and assemble the Lutradur prints you have prepared. Now choose where you would like these images – play and move them around until you have a pleasing balance to your work, referring to the printed images you used before. It is important that they complement each other, and the background. Remember, less is more. Three images are more than enough as your stitching will add and complement your work, creating balance.

∧ *Canterbury* (detail).

The photo (right) shows how I assembled all the various components of my work to produce my final piece.

1. This shape was taken from the top of the pillar and digitised using embroidery software. It was then stitched onto Lutradur which had been previously printed with an image of the pillar as a background.

2. Pillar image, printed onto Lutradur, and applied to the background with free machine embroidery.

3. This background was coloured, then screen printed.

4. Lutradur printed with my computer image.

5. This image was again printed onto Lutradur and applied with free machine embroidery.

6. The lettering and figures were digitised and applied as a final application when the panel was assembled.

The streets ring out

For every soul that

thought and felt

and passed through

sickness and strength

MELTING POINT
Learning to layer with wax and dammar

If you don't have encaustic medium to hand, you could try this out using plain beeswax. If you're a beekeeper, perfect – otherwise, a beeswax candle would suffice. It will have a lower melting point than encaustic medium, and your finished piece will be less durable over the long term, but fun to try, and a great way to discover if encaustic painting really is for you.

Julie-Ann Wrathall

In this workshop, we will be looking at ways to fuse layers of encaustic medium (beeswax and dammar resin) with mixed media and found objects to create textural, dreamy blends, full of translucency and interesting shape and pattern. Once you understand the basic principles of encaustic wax painting, it becomes as limitless as your imagination.

This workshop is designed to show you just a few of the ways to paint with encaustic wax. Once the basics are mastered, you can experiment and break the rules to your heart's content.

'Encaustic' comes from the Greek word for 'to burn', and it's the process of heating beeswax that categorises it as 'encaustic'. Dammar resin is added to the beeswax to make it more durable, and to raise the melting point. Put simply: beeswax + dammar resin = encaustic medium.

MATERIALS AND EQUIPMENT

- Encaustic medium (beeswax). I use the R&F Brand of encaustic products but there are others available, or you can make your own
- Heat source such as a craft iron or hotplate
- Tin to melt your encaustic medium
- Natural-haired brushes
- Hot air gun or embossing tool
- Encausticbord, mount board or wooden art panel – I use birch or basswood panels as these are more warp-resistant
- Old piece of cardboard to protect your table

To add colour, choose materials you already have in your stash. These could include:
- Tissue paper
- Dried leaves and flowers
- Washi tape
- Cut-outs from magazines
- Fabrics
- Oil paints, oil bars, pan pastels or glitter
- R&F pigment sticks

∧ My finished piece using encaustic wax techniques explained in this workshop.

Fusing

Fusing is critical to the structure of your finished painting. You will be bonding one layer of encaustic medium to another, to another. Don't get too concerned about the thickness of your encaustic, or the texture. You will learn as you go, and find what textures you like best.

It's always best to work on a warm surface, as this will help the encaustic medium to glide on more smoothly than applying to a cold surface. On a cold surface, you will find your brush sticks as the encaustic medium is too cool to apply in a smooth molten layer.

Fusing and warming your board can be done with a variety of tools. I use a heat gun but an embossing tool or other heat sources could be used. Some will run hotter than others. You can compensate for this by using different heat settings – high, medium, low – or by holding the heat source further away from the surface of your piece.

(2)

(5)

(6)

(9)

Getting started

1. Take your encausticbord, mount board or wooden art panel. I have used encausticbord for this workshop but the rule of thumb is that it be rigid and absorbent.

2. Melt your encaustic wax medium until it is molten. Always keep your brush in contact with the wax and heat, so it stays soft and pliable.

3. Warm the board using your heat gun.

4. Using your brush, apply one layer of encaustic medium. Load your brush and apply in one stroke – from side to side. Now, load the brush again and add another stroke, beneath the first one. Continue in this way until the surface is covered. At this stage, don't get too concerned about the thickness of your encaustic medium. This is something you will learn with practice.

5. Using a heat gun, fuse the encaustic medium until it is shiny and molten. I hold mine around 4-5in (10-14cm) from the surface on a medium heat.

6. Bend down and watch the surface of the encaustic medium closely. It's good to be at eye level to enable you to see which areas have fused. Keep the heat gun moving over all areas of the board to start, and watch constantly. You might think nothing is happening while the encaustic medium builds up to its melting point, but suddenly it will turn shiny and molten. This shiny gloss effect is the point of fusion between the layers.

7. Keep the heat gun moving over the whole board until all areas have been fused.

8. To smooth out any lumps and bumps, keep the heat in that area for longer. That will level and melt the encaustic medium into a smooth layer. To keep areas of texture and interest, just give it a lighter fuse.

9. Repeat this process until you have two layers of encaustic medium on your board, around 2-3mm thick. I like to apply the encaustic medium in a different direction to the first layer, but that's not essential. This will form the base of your painting, ready for you to add your design.

Designing

To create my piece, I chose a few components including a wooden butterfly, dried flowers and washi tape, and arranged them together until I was happy with the design.

1. When you are ready to start applying the design, decide where you would like your first piece to go and warm that section of your base. Put the piece in place and then add a layer of encaustic medium on top, just enough to hold it there. Fuse that section of the picture. I would recommend using porous items and small embellishments that will sandwich and adhere well within the encaustic medium.

2. Continue this process until all your pieces are in place and you are happy with your design.

3. To create extra texture, drip and drizzle a few drops of encaustic medium onto your piece. Carefully fuse – enough to adhere, but not enough to lose the shapes.

4 I've discovered that pottery tools, such as the one shown here, are excellent for smoothing areas and creating effects.

Remember to fuse at each stage!

Adding colour

Continue to build up your painting with colour with subsequent layers. This is as limitless as your imagination! You can add on top or scratch back in while the encaustic medium is still warm and pliable.

Here's how:

a To add colour, put a tiny dab of oil paint onto your fingertip (ensure it's not too oily) and lightly rub the paint around the raised areas of the encaustic medium. If you prefer, add a light dusting of pan pastels or glitter. Give your painting a light fuse to incorporate that colour into the wax.

b To scratch the colour back in, use a sharp tool to make incisions into the encaustic medium while it is still warm and pliable.

c Take pigment sticks or oil paint and add colour into the etched areas.

d Rub the paint deep into the grooves with the tip of your finger.

e Wipe off the excess with a tissue.

f Fuse again to bond the pigments to the structure of the painting.

g You can melt blocks of encaustic paint directly onto your heat source, and apply colour with a paintbrush.

h Make your colours more translucent by adding encaustic medium. This is similar to a watercolour wash in that by adding just a little colour, a light effect is obtained.

To finish

1. Give everything a final light fuse.

2. Remove any excess encaustic medium from the edges to leave a clean, crisp finish.

3. When completely cool and hardened, buff gently with your fingertips or a soft cloth, to bring your picture up to a beautiful shine.

4. To clean your iron, simply wipe with some tissue.

I hope you have enjoyed this workshop.

Taking it further

There are many ways to take it further, including adding colour underneath the encaustic medium, within the wax or on top of the wax. You can use it in sculpture, set fire to it using shellac and create amazing abstracts where the encaustic medium settles to its own finished design. It can be used to create fine art portraiture and landscapes. For me, it has been the most exciting discovery of my art journey.

> My finished piece (detail).

TELLING THE TALE
Maggie Grey speaks to Nikki Parmenter

Q To me your work is firmly art based, using textiles as a means of execution. It is so distinctive – how did you find your path? What led you to explore the fine art route through stitch?

A My mother says that, from an early age, I used to sit at the table with my basket of crayons. I have always been surrounded by art as my maternal grandfather was an artist, author and educator. Both my parents were teachers, so it seemed natural for me to pursue a career in art education. I gained a First Class Honours Degree in Fine Art from Manchester Polytechnic, followed by an MA and a teaching qualification. I taught Art for 30 years before taking early retirement in 2016.

The key element that makes my work so distinctive? DRAWING. I love to draw, which has helped me to conquer the ability to free machine embroider. I am absolutely addicted to this technique!

I spent many years working on paper but became dissatisfied with working on a flat surface. Encouraged by my husband (who trained as a sculptor), I started to experiment with MDF in order to achieve a more robust structure and also a low relief effect. The fact that my large artworks became almost too heavy to lift, combined with the rigidity of the wooden surface, indicated a need to change direction. Two books were particularly inspirational: *Paper, Metal and Stitch* by Maggie Grey and Jane Wild, and *Fusing Fabrics* by Margaret Beal. The techniques and materials in those books were varied and exciting and opened a whole new world for me – a cornucopia of materials and techniques for experiments.

I purchased my first sewing machine in 2005 and was somewhat daunted by the complexity of the machine. I eventually mastered the art of threading and sewing but had to rely on the manual to guide me through the various technical aspects of stitching. I clearly remember that my first attempt at a bonded fabric piece was a small peacock.

∧ *Garden of Eden* wallhanging. 8 × 10in (20 x 25cm). The background was stitched extensively and the foliage was made using painted funky foam. The figures of Adam and Eve were drawn on paper, photocopied onto acetate, stitched into the surface and then painted with acrylics.

Lacking formal textiles training has been advantageous as it has meant that I haven't been hindered by any 'rules', leaving me free to experiment. I am a fan of bonding fabrics – layering and fusing several layers of material together before machine stitching, to create a strong piece of fabric for a background or formed into an object.

Garden of Eden, a modestly sized 8 × 10in (20 × 25cm) wallhanging, was one of my earliest bonded fibre pieces. It depicts Adam and Eve under the apple tree, surrounded by foliage and creatures including a three-dimensional frog, a peacock and a flying fish. The figures were drawn on paper then photocopied onto acetate. I then stitched the acetate copy onto the wallhanging and painted the figures with acrylics. I have used this drawing and photocopying technique extensively as it is an excellent method of adding fine detail.

Another material which I discovered when making this piece was Funky Foam, also known as neoprene foam. A flexible sheet, it can be cut into complex shapes, incised, glued, painted and stitched. The piece *Caught in a Trap* demonstrates how effective Funky Foam can be for fashioning flowers and leaves. This piece was made to highlight the plight of Indonesian songbirds which are facing extinction. The birds were hand embroidered.

∧ *Garden of Eden* (detail). The versatile nature of Funky Foam can be seen clearly here. The leaves were incised with a ballpoint pen, then painted and glued onto the surface of the fabric.

In 2018, I made a wallhanging based on the damage to the Great Barrier Reef by pollution, global warming and plastics. For the first time, I incorporated real pieces of plastic in the work and discovered my 'plastic entrapment technique' which I have since honed and developed.

Essentially another layering technique, this involves placing a piece of clear PVC fabric on a surface and covering it with iridescent and translucent fabrics. Having been topped by another piece of PVC with a drawn image, the area is then stitched extensively with free machine embroidery. The **Bird Cameo** work, based on Victorian scraps and spring flowers, also uses this method. One of a series of pieces looking at bird imagery, this depicts a peace dove with a flower in her beak. **Home Birds** is another work in the series, symbolising spring and birth.

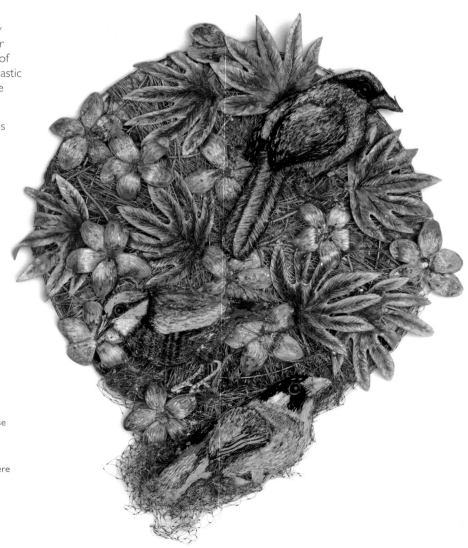

> *Caught in a Trap.* 16 x 18in (40 x 48cm). The base is a flower-arranger's copper hoop. I wrapped embroidery thread around the hoop to create a spider's web surface onto which hand-embroidered birds, foam flowers and leaves were applied. The foliage was painted with acrylics.

I have developed a fascination with recycling and upcycling, and seeing how unusual materials can be incorporated into my work. These have included hosepipes, recycled plastics, rope, washers, tomato purée tubes, insulation pipes and boards, woodworkers' biscuits (used for attaching wooden joints together), chicken wire, bandages, handmade felt, non-slip matting, hula-hoops, broken jewellery, copper wire hoops, spray paint, ballcocks, car wheel trims, toothpicks, curtain hooks and strings of LED lights … anything goes!

> *Home Birds*. 15 x 24in (39 x 60cm). The birds were based on Victorian scraps and were created using the plastic entrapment method, as were the bees. The foliage to the left was monoprinted on fabric and painted. I fashioned the nest with hand felting which incorporated sari silks. The polystyrene eggs were collaged with gold Joss paper.

∨ *Caught in a Trap* (detail). The embroidery thread, which was wrapped around the hoop, is clearly visible, and provided an excellent base.

> *Love Train* (detail) love birds. The birds were drawn on paper, photocopied onto acetate and painted with acrylic. Embellishments, including sequins and beads, were applied.

Q Your larger pieces explore themes from the religious to the secular, with folk tales and fables featuring strongly. Where do you find these sources of inspiration? Are they responsible for the vibrant colours that characterise your work?

A I love vibrant colour and, several years ago, produced a series of pieces inspired by Indian art. The colour, texture, and heavily embellished aspect of this style of art led me to use strong, rich hues and jewelled elements, which I still incorporate into my work.

I never lack inspiration! My influences rarely come from the study of textile art and artists. Each piece made is centred on subject matter rather than a specific technique. I credit my parents, and summer holidays abroad, for giving me the experience of visiting art galleries, cathedrals, ruins, sites of interest, capital cities, stunning scenery and fascinating architecture. Literature, stories, religion, mythology, flora and fauna, symbolism – in fact anything that grabs my attention and imagination is brought to bear.

Love Train demonstrates the research into a particular theme across a range of cultures. The initial starting point was some First World War silk postcards, sent home by the troops to their wives and sweethearts. Another inspiration was my mother's wedding veil, which she gave to me to use in my work. Although it was not in the best condition, there were enough lace flowers to cut out and incorporate into the piece. My aim was to create a 'Miss Havisham' style textile which looked delicate and fragile, hence the torn netting which holds the piece together. The bride's face was painted in a style reminiscent of Alphonse Mucha, and more Mucha women feature lower down the veil.

Featuring cherubs, sentimental Victorian scraps and doves as well as roses, the piece includes Eve, Aphrodite and Kamadeva, the Indian God of Love. Two white butterflies which symbolise marital harmony in Chinese culture flutter around the base of the veil and, nearby, there are two jewelled lovebirds.

> *Love Train* (detail) Mucha head. The head in profile was drawn on paper, photocopied onto acetate and painted with acrylic.

> *Love Train*. Height 110in x (widest point) 54in (277 x 134cm). The piece was constructed using white netting with individual panels attached, portraying references to love and romance inspired by mythology, history and literature. The images were drawn on paper, photocopied onto acetate then painted with acrylics. The effect I was striving to achieve was a 'Miss Havisham-inspired' piece with a slightly decayed, decadent air.

Q Do you begin with a paper and paint design or do you 'see' the finished piece in your mind's eye and work towards it? Does it develop as the materials dictate and do you allow yourself to be diverted from the plan?

A I start with a theme and rarely plan on paper. I have a vague notion as to how the finished piece might look, but am more focused on its individual components. After the initial stimulus, my thoughts and ideas evolve and develop over time as I research the subject in greater depth.

As an example, the plastic entrapment pieces for my wallhanging *The Sea Goddess, Sedna* will be assembled as a large 7ft (about 2 metres) tall composition. Sedna was an Inuit woman, tricked into marrying a man disguised as a bird, who took her to live on a deserted island. Sedna's father, on a visit, killed the birdman when he saw that his daughter was unhappy. They tried to return home in his kayak but the friends of the birdman caused a great storm by flapping their wings. Sedna's father threw her overboard to appease the birds, but the attack continued. Sedna clung to the boat and, afraid that the kayak would capsize, her father chopped her fingers off. She sank to the bottom of the ocean. Sedna became a powerful spirit and her fingers turned into whales, fish, and sea creatures. This myth is so inspirational and evocative.

∧ *The Sea Goddess, Sedna* (detail). 23in diameter (58cm). Based on the work of Ernst Haeckel. There is no drawing on this piece and the linear aspects were achieved by free machine embroidery. Plastic elements, including toothpicks and cellophane, were assembled to form a decorative repeat pattern, referencing Haeckel's sea urchins, corals and starfish.

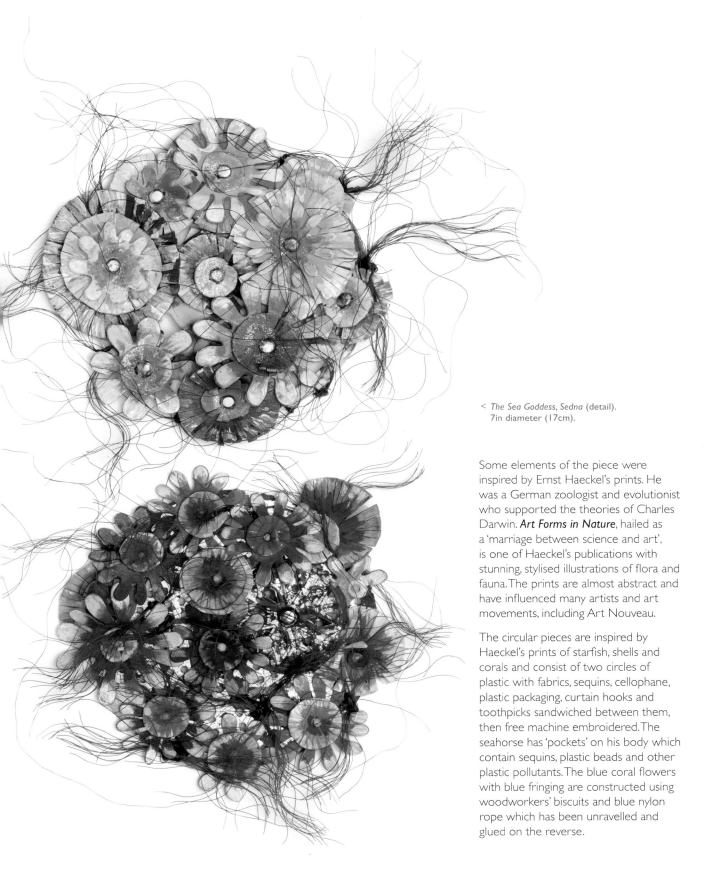

< *The Sea Goddess, Sedna* (detail).
7in diameter (17cm).

Some elements of the piece were inspired by Ernst Haeckel's prints. He was a German zoologist and evolutionist who supported the theories of Charles Darwin. **Art Forms in Nature**, hailed as a 'marriage between science and art', is one of Haeckel's publications with stunning, stylised illustrations of flora and fauna. The prints are almost abstract and have influenced many artists and art movements, including Art Nouveau.

The circular pieces are inspired by Haeckel's prints of starfish, shells and corals and consist of two circles of plastic with fabrics, sequins, cellophane, plastic packaging, curtain hooks and toothpicks sandwiched between them, then free machine embroidered. The seahorse has 'pockets' on his body which contain sequins, plastic beads and other plastic pollutants. The blue coral flowers with blue fringing are constructed using woodworkers' biscuits and blue nylon rope which has been unravelled and glued on the reverse.

∨ *The Sea Goddess, Sedna*
(detail). 7.5in diameter
(19cm) including fringing.
Flowers made with
woodworkers' biscuits.

Q You work big – do you have a spacious studio and how do you store finished pieces before an exhibition?

A I would love to have a spacious studio! I live in a typical three-bedroomed house which has a modest conservatory where I store my materials on shelves and where I stitch. The garage is full of work.

Fortunately, most of my pieces are wallhangings which can be rolled up and put into bags. My work is quite robust and can take a certain amount of rough handling. I am relaxed about people touching the pieces and, if part of a piece comes away, I simply glue or stitch it back together.

Many of my projects are large in scale and take several months to complete. I accumulate work for each project and store it in large bags until I am ready to put everything together. This involves spreading all the pieces on the floor and taking photographs of different compositions.

Q Your work appeals to such a wide range of art lovers and you have a fantastic solo exhibition record at prestigious venues. Do you mostly work for exhibitions – what about commissions or pieces just for you?

A I produce work because I am totally addicted to textiles and mixed media. I have a huge amount of work as I am very loath to part with any of it, unless it's an older piece. Some of my work can take several months to complete so I become very attached to it. In addition, I would need to charge a high figure to reflect the hours spent on each piece.

∨ *The Sea Goddess, Sedna*
(detail). 13 x 8in (33 x 20cm).

Retiring from full-time teaching in 2016, I had to make a decision as to whether I wanted to create a market for my work or focus on exhibiting and teaching. I chose the latter. I give talks to various groups and societies, often leading to a workshop. I also tutor textile schools and write articles and projects for magazines and online platforms.

It's very flattering to receive a request for a commission; the problem for me is that I've already researched and made the original. There isn't as much creative exploration to be found in replicating it. I always strive to make the next piece more adventurous and successful than the previous one.

I have exhibited at some well-known venues and always take my inspiration from their artefacts. I enjoy providing 'Meet the Artist' sessions to engage with the public. Workshops often run alongside the show and help participants experience some of the techniques. I hope my work appeals to a range of audiences and that the diverse subject matter (to quote my non-artistic son) is 'accessible to all'.

The *Della Robbia Vase*, based on the collection of ceramics in the permanent collection at the Williamson Art Gallery in Birkenhead, UK, was one of a number of pieces in a solo show at the Williamson in 2019. The original Della Robbia factory operated in Florence in the 16th century producing terracotta pieces such as wall plaques, roundels, altar pieces and fountains in white, blue, yellow and green colours, often decorated with floral swags and fruits. The technique was rediscovered in 1896 by Harold Rathbone in Birkenhead. My vase was made with bonded fabrics glued on a papier-mâché vase and decorated with motifs.

> *Della Robbia Vase*. Height 15in, circumference 20in (38 x 51cm). The vase was covered with fused fabric with attached free machine embroidered elements. These were taken from the Della Robbia ceramics in the Williamson Art Gallery and included a cherub, a cockatoo and floral elements.

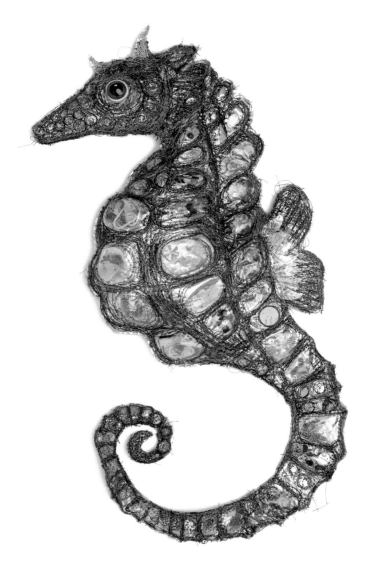

∧ *The Goddess, Sedna* (detail) seahorse. 18 x 9in (23 x 46cm). I used the plastic entrapment technique and sandwiched plastic and cellophane elements inside the seahorse, then applied free machine embroidery. I added a number of plastic 'pockets' to the surface into which I stitched sequins, plastic knitting pins and other items.

∨ *The Goddess, Sedna* (detail) coral.

Q How important is it to belong to an exhibiting group and how does it differ from the solo shows? When working towards an exhibition, how do you organise your time?

A I think that there are huge benefits in belonging to an exhibiting group. I am a member of the north-west England based Textile 21, a group of wonderfully supportive artists who meet to share ideas, critiques and practical sessions. Zoom meetings have been invaluable during lockdown.

I am also a member of Glossop Embroiderers' Guild and am able to draw on the vast stitching expertise of my fellow members and experience talks by other practitioners.

A solo exhibition allows me to showcase my work and explain my techniques and influences to visitors. As much of my work is large in scale, I value the opportunity to see the pieces in a gallery setting with sufficient space to display them. It is very satisfying and exciting to display the variety of work that I produce, from smaller wallhangings through three-dimensional pieces, to the much larger and complex pieces.

When planning for an exhibition, I ensure I have several months' notice, so have a timetable mapped out in my head. Pieces are created to be specific to the gallery and I spend some time researching the artefacts on display there. An example of this is my exhibition *Floralia* at Gawthorpe Hall in Padiham (Burnley, Lancashire, England). The Hall houses the world-famous Gawthorpe Textiles Collection and several of my exhibits there take imagery directly from the collection.

Q What does a typical day in your workshop look like? Do you ever have 'stitcher's block' and, if so, how do you overcome it?

A There isn't really a typical day. I took early retirement in 2016 and can now create my own timetable. I check my diary regularly for talks and workshops, and then plan when I will be able to fit in some stitching time. Any administration is cleared in the morning, leaving time for working. I have recently started to offer online workshops and promote these by advertising them on my Facebook page: *www.facebook. com/nikkiparmenterartworks*

I usually have several projects in progress so, on the rare occasion when I might be feeling frustrated with a particular element, I simply put it to one side and work on something else.

> *The Goddess, Sedna* (detail) coral. 24 x 11in (60 x 28cm). The stitching is spontaneous and fluid, and I responded to the materials trapped between the pieces of plastic to inform the direction and colour of the stitch. My intention was to create a piece with an organic feel.

Q Have you found that the current situation, with its focus on staying put, has helped the creative process or dampened it? I think it has been particularly difficult for exhibiting artists, both from the financial and the creative aspects.

A During the pandemic, I have worked constantly and consistently. The forced lockdown gave me the opportunity to immerse myself in my creative practice and has kept me sane.

Throughout lockdown, people have been searching for stimulation and ideas online and, as a result, the development of Zoom has transformed the way that I connect with my audience. Rather than giving a face-to-face lecture, I have devised a PowerPoint presentation, delivered as a screen-share lecture. This has given me the opportunity to add contextual detail which just wouldn't work during a 'live' talk. I take my audience on a Zoom tour through time to visit the people and places that have caught my imagination: Matisse, Yeats, Dürer, Leonardo, Ancient Greece, Italy, Japan, Holland, Persia, B&Q . . .

My online workshops are delivered via Zoom which has meant that I can attract participants from around the world. This is a very new and exciting development which I would never have thought possible a year ago.

I am hoping to resume my Masterclass workshops with Janome (who support me in my creative practice) at their HQ in Greater Manchester in the near future.

∧ *The Sea Goddess, Sedna* (detail). Coral including teeth-flossing elements.

< *Della Robbia Vase* (detail).

Chris Gray

I have been a stitcher for as long as I can remember. All of the women in my family were skilled with knitting pins, crochet hooks and sewing needles. Being the kind of child who needed to be involved, I was given hooks and needles and gently encouraged to have a go.

So began my stitching journey but at the same time, I also learnt the more masculine skills, using various tools in the garden sheds belonging to uncles and grandfathers. I was even given a small toolkit of my own – much to the disgust of my mother who was trying to turn me into a little lady. No chance! Thus I am as at home with wood, metal and wire as I am with thread, fabric and yarn. I call that a very good beginning.

Early academic studies introduced me to history and took me from about 3500 BCE up to AD 410. I had little knowledge of what happened after the fall of the Roman Empire until, in 2015, a book fell off the shelf in a local bookshop, and I became absolutely hooked on the medieval period. My interest continues with my knowledge growing all the while. I have even taken to holidaying in France to research 12th-century sculpture.

∧ This is one of a series of 15 different tile block prints with many layers of hand stitch around it. I used hand-dyed threads in silk and cotton with metallic threads in and around. Of course, nothing is finished without beads, is it? The whole piece was sprinkled liberally with sizes 11 and 15 beads.

After seeing Welsh paving tiles in the National Museum in Cardiff, Wales, I had some medieval tile blocks cut from drawings I had made. I have used this set of 24 tiles over and over in many projects, including my workshop for this book. Printing and then stitching — by hand and machine — is such an enjoyable part of my life. I use the blocks to print with acrylic paints as well as to make embossed pieces in a much-loved cast-iron book press.

Over the last few years, I have exhibited my medieval pieces at shows in the UK and France, and have taken my blocks out to group workshops for other people to play with and enjoy. I have also made a number of small printed and stitched books, just for my own pleasure.

< A page from my Romanesque sketchbook. It is an *ouroboros* — a creature that eats its own tail. I find these weird creatures utterly fascinating and, hopefully, this one will be a carved linoprint first of all before being translated into a piece of stitching, possibly trapunto.

Recently, I find myself focusing on my hand embroidery which I stitch around the tile prints. A distinct style has emerged. This is now being expanded upon and I am currently working on a book that will be full of projects with this kind of stitching. I am hoping it will be published in 2021. My previous book *Stitching Magic – Beginning the Journey* (now out of print) was published back in 2013.

You can see my work in progress, experiments and general babbling on my blog, Textile Butterfly.

www.chris-gray-textile-art.blogspot.com
www.facebook.com/profile.php?id=555382986

∧ A page from a printed and stitched small book. I used a block print onto fabric with hand stitch around and a rubber stamp on the opposite page. You'll see that the background is the same medieval text that is used in the workshop in this book, but printed onto deli-paper. Pieces of gold leaf were added for a luxurious finish and painted pennants add colour around the edges.

Maggie Grey

I had an accidental introduction to textiles. Always keen on drawing and painting, I mistakenly purchased a book on landscapes that turned out to be machine embroidery on painted fabrics. I loved making these and it led me to a City & Guilds course where there was a shocking discovery – it included hand embroidery. After initial resistance, I came to enjoy this (in the end).

Having completed the course, I practised on some unsuspecting students while conducting day schools and giving talks; this led to teaching City & Guilds classes at a local college. A passionate campaigner for design and an early adapter (thanks to husband, Clive) of the use of the home computer paint programs, I was introduced to the late Valerie Campbell-Harding and together we taught computer design at Summer Schools and residential courses.

∨ *The Book of Covid*. A 'visual' diary representing our time of enforced isolation. Some of the Facebook quotes from my *Lockdown* panel on page 2 crept in here too. Limiting myself to a dark colour scheme, walnut ink with occasional watercolour was mostly used, plus a restrained amount of glitz to cheer things up.

There was such demand that Clive was roped in to help. He threw in his job and together we travelled to far-distant lands, tutoring Summer Schools and forums in Australia, New Zealand and Canada, and working with a regular group in the USA. Teaching continued in the UK on all aspects of stitch and design and this led to my writing numerous books for Batsford, often with friends Val Campbell-Harding and Jane Wild.

When Val decided to move on from editorship of *Embroidery* magazine, I was delighted to succeed her, a big commitment but a very enjoyable one.

The next venture was a thriving distance learning business with both design and stitch on the syllabus. I had students from all over the world and they would send in their work for assessment. With such a long waiting list, Clive and I decided to stop all the assessments and produce the lessons on a quarterly basis instead. Then it occurred to us to ask other tutors to write lessons and, twelve years ago, it turned into the internet magazine *Workshop on the Web* which ran for many years and brought us great pleasure and lots of friends around the world. Fiona Edwards joined us and was a great partner in this venture, making it run very smoothly. The advent of d4daisy Books gave me more control over the content and much greater scope for the books.

The internet is still a powerful influence and has been especially so in lockdown. My *Book of Covid* is a tribute to Facebook, where friends keep me focused and make me laugh a lot.

www.greytech.org.uk/maggiegrey
www.facebook.com/maggie.grey.92

> *Binary Humanity.* This piece was made for the Cyber Fyber exhibition (2009) in the USA, which celebrated the internet. The notes around the edge came from contributors to my blog. The faces and hands are made from cast paper, metal shim and stitch. Some of the faces were made by my friend Jane Wild. This is the piece that provided the inspiration for the *Lockdown* piece on page 2.

Jan Horrox

I was introduced to handicrafts while growing up with my mum in the Second World War, when knitting, sewing and makeovers were an essential part of life during times of rationing.

In 1958, I took a two-year intermediate course at Norwich Art School. I followed this with ten years of working at various jobs while bringing up my family. These included working as a stylist with a top photographer, as a machinist for Charles Fox Theatrical Costumiers, screen-printing T-shirts and being an assistant in Sotheby's photographic studio. These gave me a taste for art and design. In 1970, I returned to full-time education, taking a fashion/textile diploma at Walthamstow Art School, UK, specialising in knitwear. My final show featured experimental airbrushed knitwear combined with fabrics.

After leaving college, I started producing and selling my own collection of knitwear in high-end stores in the UK, the USA and Japan, mainly through trade fairs in the UK and New York. I also taught knitwear design at Somerset Art College.

In the late 1980s, I opened a shop in Haverstock Hill called 'Softwear' where we sold knitwear, including my own and other designer makes. We also sold a unique range of beautiful yarns and accessories plus knitted sculpture and hangings. I employed other young designers in the shop, so it became a great hub for ideas. I was still producing mainly machine knitwear although I did dabble with intarsia hand knits. During the 1980s, I designed picture sweaters and complicated geometric patterns.

< This doll is called *Laurel*, the evergreen shrub and source of bay leaves. I have used my own hand-dyed fabrics and created the root pattern by using household bleach, a technique taken from the workshop by Mary McIntosh in WOWbook 05. The features are all earthy colours with hand-embroidered accents. Her hair is made from ribbing from an old jumper and dyed scrim makes the skirt. I often stuff my dolls with wool-based fibre to keep their natural content.

My knitwear business continued into the 2000s although it became mainly retail around the millennium. At that time, I was working in 'Waterside', a wonderful studio in a wharf building on the Thames in Rotherhithe. This was a craft co-op of around 18 people and I was here for about 12 years. We held regular open studios which proved successful locally. I had a large beamed studio with a view of Tower Bridge, all at a low cost, and made many great friendships.

In about 2003, while selling and exhibiting my knitwear at the Knitting & Stitching Show, I was introduced to cloth dolls by some American designers. I was very attracted to cloth dolls as they incorporated many techniques that interested me. I loved the small scale, after years of transporting vans of knitwear around the country!

I attended some workshops with Ray Slater and made my first dolls. Soon, I was making my own designs and patterns. I set up a supplies business as, at the time, it was impossible to find these anywhere in the UK. I now sell my individual art dolls through commission, social media and my website. I enjoy creating my own fabrics with dyes and embroidery, then adding embellishments. I run weekend workshops in Glastonbury and very much enjoy teaching, focusing on showing the basic techniques while aiding my students to create something individual.

In a world where climate change and a global pandemic have greatly affected our lives in a negative way, I am working with natural and re-purposed materials on a theme of preserving the natural elements of our environment. The dolls shown here and in my workshop are all designed with this idea in mind. They all measure around 14in (35.5cm) tall and are made from the same pattern, with changes made to the joints and embellishing techniques.

I have written two books, *An Introduction To Making Cloth Dolls*, published in 2010, and *Making Fantasy Cloth Dolls*, which was published in 2012. A compilation book: *How To Make Cloth Dolls* was published recently.

www.janhorrox.co.uk

∨ *Nutmeg* (left) – one of my favourite spices and evocative of good times such as baking at Christmas. This doll is made with hand-dyed fabrics, and a root pattern created with bleach dye removal. I have couched scraps of textured yarn over the root patterns. The joints are stained wooden beads with a skirt made from dyed scrim and fabric leaves. Her face is partly embroidered.

∨ Our bee population is in grave danger throughout the world and I designed this Queen Bee doll as an addition to the earth dolls – to remind us that bees are an essential element of our environment. Her body is machine embroidered silk with wooden bead joints and her face has been embroidered with one strand of sewing cotton and her wings are made from a sheet of Angelina.

Amo House

As long as there is a needle involved, I'm in a happy place. Even if the project happens to be paper or mixed media, I'll always look at ways to add stitch or thread somewhere. If I'm not being 'arty', I'm still creating by knitting, crocheting or sewing panels. These may not use the same thought processes as my other projects, but they keep the fingers busy. They also allow my mind a little quiet place to think which may then lead to a more 'arty' idea. I have, sadly, had a few blank moments during these strange times.

I have been sewing and knitting since my grandmother taught me as a small child and I love being surrounded by fabrics and yarns. The sound of pulling thread through fabric is soothing to me, and the rhythm of making stitches quite mesmerising. Just watching others do this is calming.

< Watercolour snowdrops set into a mixed media background. The surround is text, wax, lace, buttons and thread. This piece is the last of a series I created for a Spring exhibition. I love the soft palette and haziness the wax gives.

∨ A little collection of insects made with beads and fabrics. In life, beetles can be very fanciful and beautiful things so nothing can be too outlandish, even if you totally make them up. Charity shop jewellery finds are a great place to start with these.

I love being a mixed media artist and all the clutter that brings. After completing my City & Guilds in Creative Techniques – Textiles in 2012, I started to explore different areas such as art quilts, bead embroidery and 3D dolls. I have more boxes, drawers and cupboards full of materials and fabric (plus a few forgotten gems) than I care to admit.

Often, I've dyed my own fabric and threads, made eco prints and recreated fabrics by combining scraps of fabric and yarns. Although the natural world is a huge influence, my work is beginning to lean more towards the abstract, but I still like to include my favourites – ammonites and moths. I have exhibited in several exhibitions in the past and enjoy the Open Studio events through Dorset Art Weeks and meeting people interested in textile work.

This past year has been a challenge for most of us and has either led to no creativity at all or a fair bit more than normal. I am lucky to have a room (or two) all to myself and my 'mess'. During the first lockdown, I was unable to settle to anything and spent too much time just wandering in and out of my workroom. In trying to kick my creativity into starting position, I have tried to not buy anything new unless it is totally necessary to my work, or a staple product such as matt medium, or one of my favourite colours of ink or paint. The challenge to find a way of using something when it's unearthed or of looking for an alternative is something I want to explore more. All those 'special' things which have been saved over the years need to be used – and I'm going to try my hardest to achieve this.

∧ Many pages of mixed media and found objects combined into little collections of interest. The covers of the book are made from a tin which I have rusted and aged. This is a great way of using all those tiny bits that you just can't bear to part with and throw away. I like spending time matching them up into cohesive groups.

Sue Munday

As a child, I was always encouraged to stitch by my mother and grandmother; both accomplished seamstresses and knitters. My grandmother would turn everything inside out, just to make sure it was as neat on the inside as it was on the outside. I also loved to draw and paint and would spend hours quite happily in these activities. As an only child, this was a very useful way to fill time. I studied art at school but my career initially took a different turn – secretarial school followed by working at a training centre for lecturers in design and construction. Time went by during which I married, had children and ran a business, so it was not until much later that I had the opportunity to do something for myself.

While in the process of moving to West Sussex, I visited an excellent exhibition of City & Guilds creative courses at Windsor, Berkshire, UK, and was overwhelmed by the standard of work and creativity – under the tutelage of Jan Beaney and Jean Littlejohn. A City & Guilds creative embroidery course was discovered near to my new home, and I spent four years studying, during which I found a passion for machine embroidery. At the end of the course, I began teaching City & Guilds embroidery and machine embroidery at Fareham College, then Northbrook College and Missenden Abbey.

I also had the opportunity to teach freelance, covering workshops and talks for groups and the Embroiderers' Guild, and demonstrating at shows around the country. As one teaches, so one learns from one's students. While demonstrating at Brighton Conference Centre, Janome UK, asked me if I would partner with them, using their machines and software.

Tamarisk Textiles, of which I am a member, was formed here in West Sussex in 1998. We exhibit our work around Chichester, in the Oxmarket, and the Assembly Rooms. Due to changes in our lives, we are now a smaller group, but still gather together and encourage each other.

I am now semi-retired and have the opportunity to produce my own work and work as part of a small group of friends and textile artists. Using the internet, I keep in touch with fellow textile artists; it does have its uses!

< This piece came about while attending a workshop with Alison Hulme. I worked with Thermofax screen prints of fern, grasses and poppies. These were stitched into the printed piece using free machine stitching together with digitised poppy shapes. Finally, I stitched the digitised design over the printed images of the poppies.

My influences are found in the world around me – landscapes, flowers, shapes, colours, texture, and architecture, history and archaeology.

Currently, I am working towards a piece relating to the Gallic Warrior who was found locally and is the subject of a wonderful exhibition in the Chichester Museum in 2020/21. He was buried with his sword and helmet, three vessels at his head with another at his feet.

www.facebook.com/sue.munday1

^ Detail of *Tulip*, one of three images. I took three sections of a picture and enlarged them. I chose a previously dyed piece of synthetic fabric as the background and this was bonded onto a piece of S80 Vilene. The shape was transferred and I free machined each section. As I stitched, the Vilene distorted, adding movement.

∧ *They Watch Over Us.*
Using papers, print,
inks, stencils and pan
pastels within the layers
of encaustic, helps to
create a truly ethereal
feel to this painting.

Julie-Ann Wrathall

I am a professional fine artist based in the UK who specialises in the ancient art of encaustic wax painting. However, I haven't always been an artist. As a child, I never put down a pencil but was encouraged to take cookery over art at school. Cookery was apparently far more 'practical' and art – only a hobby! So my art practice stopped, and I fell into corporate work. I only started drawing and painting again in January 2011.

In September 2011, I entered a competition on a whim and was selected as one of 80 artists to work on a project at the Tate Modern in London. That was it. Winning that competition gave me the confidence to pursue my dream of working in the arts, something that hadn't seemed possible previously. My corporate background wasn't wasted, however, and it gave me much technical and business know-how which enabled me to set up my own art company.

I experienced my first ever encaustic wax painting at an exhibition back in 2012, and I say experienced – it stopped me dead in my tracks. I can picture it now, hanging at the very top of the exhibition stand. It was a blend of blue and silver shimmers and texture that moved me to my core. I was mesmerised and stared at it, desperate to touch it. I had to find out how to paint like that and promptly booked myself onto a workshop to find out.

I fell in love with the medium and have never gone back to my previously used materials. I feel there is something extra special about the texture, the application, and the way you can build limitless layers with the translucency of each layer shining through.

I started sharing my work at local events and through Herts. Open Studios, and found that others were as intrigued about encaustic wax as I was, and wanted to know more. Over time, I began sharing my techniques, which involved running classes, demos and workshops in some truly amazing locations. I must have shared these skills with hundreds, maybe thousands, of people over the last few years.

There have been many twists and turns along the way, but I believe we all need art in our lives. Encaustic brings a little known layer to that, so my mission is to share it as widely as possible!

Moving forward, I am now focusing on creating art and no longer run workshops or courses, but I still love to help people on their encaustic journey, especially as information around this medium is so limited. I've created a series of online courses to help people working with encaustic medium. I have received some great feedback and get such a buzz when people send me a picture of their set-up, or their first creation, to know that they are enjoying it as much as I do.

www.artyheaven.com
www.facebook.com/julieannsgallery

< *Windows to the Soul.* This is an example of the detail you can create using layers of encaustic paint. I love the effects and depth of the skin tones where the layers are fused and blended together quite loosely, contrasting with the fine detail of her eyes and features.

∨ *Taraxacum Glow.* One of my early pieces using the most basic of equipment: an old decorating brush, an iron, a heat gun, encaustic medium and oil paints. I added the dried leaf and cut-out butterfly. The straight lines were produced with the edge of my iron. Simple but effective.